TEACHER'S BOOK

Second edition

Karen Saxby
Emily Hird

Cambridge University Press
www.cambridge.org/elt

Cambridge English Language Assessment
www.cambridgeenglish.org

Information on this title: www.cambridge.org/9781316617199

First published 2011 © Cambridge University Press & Assessment
Second edition 2017 © Cambridge University Press & Assessment and UCLES

20 19 18 17 16 15 14 13 12 11 10 9

Printed in Great Britain by CPI Group (UK) Ltd, Croydon CR0 4YY

A catalogue record for this publication is available from the British Library

ISBN 978-1-316-61717-5 Student's Book with online activities and Home Fun booklet 4
ISBN 978-1-316-61719-9 Teacher's Book with Audio 4
ISBN 978-1-316-61723-6 Presentation plus 4

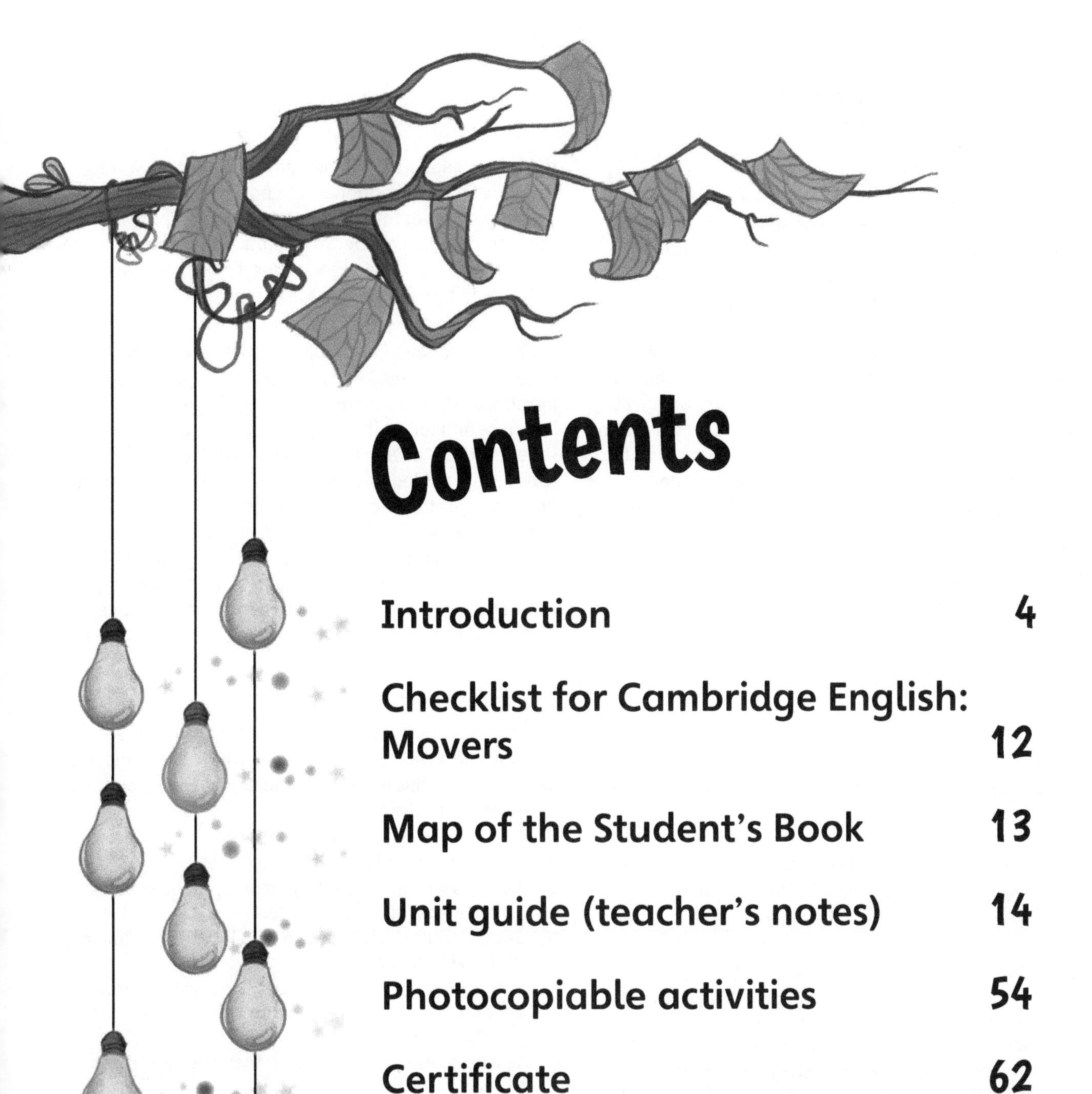

Contents

= Value		= Let's say! pages	
= Song		= Audio	
= Test tasks for Movers		= Interactive activity	
= Practice for Movers		= Home FUN booklet	
= Let's have fun! pages		= Online activities	
= Let's speak! pages			

Introduction

Welcome to *Storyfun*!

Storyfun is a series of six books written for young learners aged between 6 and 12 years. The series provides story-based preparation for the Cambridge English: Young Learners tests (YLE). Each Student's Book contains eight stories with activities that include vocabulary and grammar tasks, puzzles, games, poems, songs and an exploration of the story 'value' (for example, an appreciation of nature, the importance of friendship). The Teacher's Books provide detailed suggestions on how to approach the storytelling, together with clear instructions for guiding learners through the unit. With a variety of flexible resources, each unit in *Storyfun* is designed to provide approximately three to four hours of class time.

Why stories?

Storyfun aims to provide an opportunity for language practice by engaging learners' interest in stories.

Research has shown that meaningful and imaginative stories can motivate learning because learners:

- engage with the text and their imaginations.
- learn vocabulary with repetition of key words in the text and pictures.
- are exposed to repeated rhyme and sound patterns and accurate pronunciation.
- develop deeper social understanding by relating to characters and events in the story.
- actively engage listening skills as they predict, hypothesise and await outcomes.

Points to remember for effective learning:

- Story-reading should be interactive (teacher and learners). It should involve pointing, describing and discussing how the story relates to the real world.
- Learners will engage with a story more if they are encouraged to 'work out' the meaning, for example, why learners think characters did something or how characters felt at a certain moment and, of course, what the story 'value' is.
- Learners benefit from more than one reading or hearing of a story. At least one reading should be read/heard right the way through from beginning to end without interruption.

For more information about stories in language learning, go to

Why Cambridge English: Young Learners (YLE)?

The stories have been written to reflect the different language levels and topic areas of the Cambridge English: Starters, Movers and Flyers tests and to appeal to the target-reader age groups. The language of the stories is exploited in activities that check comprehension, teach key vocabulary and grammar, practise all four language skills (reading, writing, listening and speaking) and give learners an opportunity to familiarise themselves with the nature and format of the Cambridge English: Young Learners tests. The optional *Let's have fun!* and *Let's speak!* sections at the back of the books also provide opportunities for collaborative learning and test speaking practice. The *Let's say!* pages support early pronunciation skills, building from sounds to sentences.

There are two Student's Books for each test: pre-A1 (Starters), A1 (Movers) and A2 (Flyers). *Storyfun 3* gently introduces students to the Cambridge English: Movers language and topics through fun activities and test-style practice. Activities are carefully graded to ensure learners are guided towards the test level, with frequent opportunities to build up their language and skills. *Storyfun 4* provides full practice of all the Cambridge English: Movers test tasks. By the end of *Storyfun* levels 3 and 4, constant recycling of language and test task types ensures learners are fully prepared for the Cambridge English: Movers test.

Who is *Storyfun* for?

Storyfun has been written for teachers and young learners of English in a wide variety of situations. It is suitable for:

- learners in this age group who enjoy reading and listening to stories
- large and small groups of learners
- monolingual and multilingual classes
- learners who are beginning to prepare to take the Cambridge English: Movers test
- young learners who need to develop their vocabulary, grammar and language
- young learners keen to discuss social values, develop collaborative learning skills and build confidence for the Movers Speaking paper
- teachers who wish to develop their learners' literacy skills

What are the key features of *Storyfun 4*?

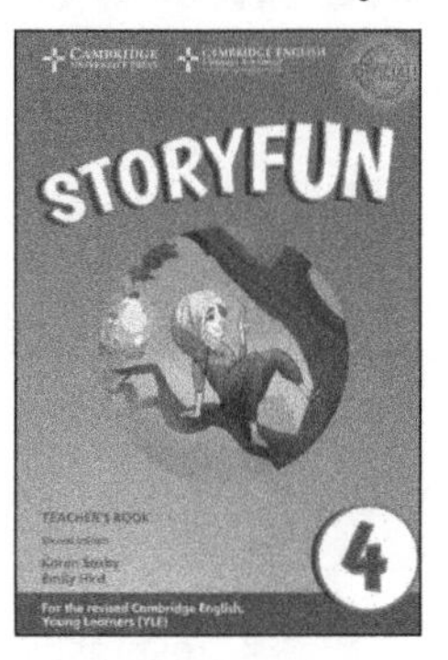

Student's Book

- eight imaginative and motivating stories
- fun, interactive, creative and meaningful activities
- activities similar to task types found in all three parts (Reading and Writing, Listening and Speaking) of the Cambridge English: Movers test

- an introduction to Cambridge English: Movers grammar and vocabulary
- extension activities *Let's have fun!*, further speaking practice *Let's speak!* and an early pronunciation focus *Let's say!*
- unit-by-unit word list

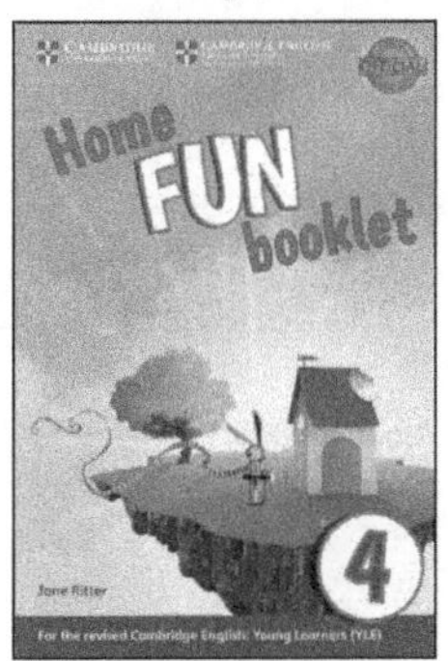

Home FUN booklet

- fun activities for learners to try at home
- 'self-assessment' activities that build learners' confidence and encourage autonomy
- a Cambridge English: Movers picture dictionary
- *Let's have fun!* pages to encourage learners to use English in the wider world
- answers, audio and additional support found online by using the access code at the front of the book

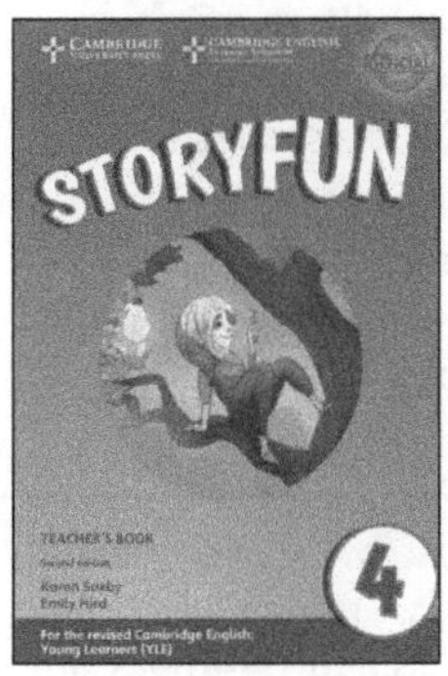

Teacher's Book with Audio

- a map of the Student's Book (topics, grammar points and Movers test practice for each unit)
- practical step-by-step notes with suggestions for:
  - ✓ personalisation at presentation and practice stages
  - ✓ skills work: reading, writing, listening, speaking, drawing and colouring
  - ✓ pair and group work
  - ✓ puzzles, games, poems and songs
  - ✓ speaking activities and projects
  - ✓ discussion tasks to explore the story 'value'
  - ✓ recycling of language
  - ✓ incorporating digital materials into the lesson
- Cambridge English: Movers test tips
- full audioscripts
- imaginative audio recordings for stories and activities (downloadable by using the access code at the front of this book) reflective of the Cambridge English: Movers Listening test
- photocopiable pages for the Student's Book or optional extension activities
- links to online practice and the Home FUN booklet

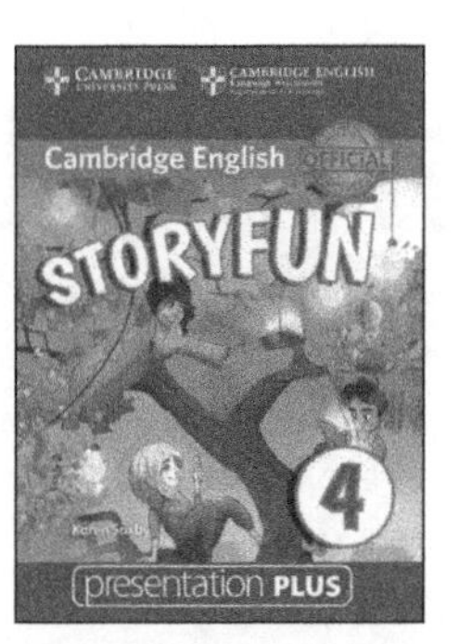

Presentation plus

- digital version of all Student's Book pages
- interactive Student's Book activities
- audio played directly from the digital page
- digital flashcards with audio
- digital slideshow of every story
- an Image carousel that provides further visuals associated with story themes
- integrated tools to make notes and highlight activities

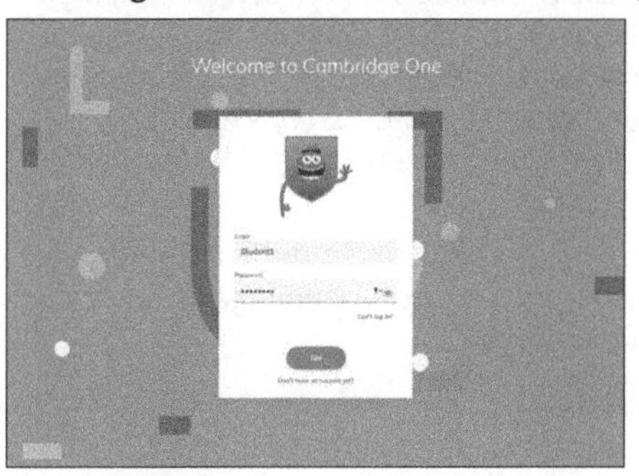

Online Practice

For the Teacher

- Presentation plus
- All audio recordings
- Additional digital resources to support your classes

For the Student

- Fun activities to practise the exam, skills and language
- All audio recordings
- Additional digital resources

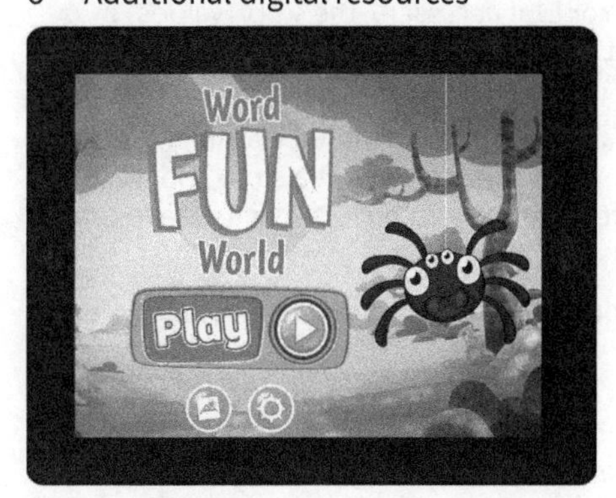

Word FUN World app

- Cambridge English: Young Learners vocabulary game
- For mobile phones and tablets

Why should we use stories in language learning classes?

There are several reasons! A good story encourages us to turn the next page and read more. We want to find out what happens next and what the main characters do and say to each other. We may feel excited, sad, afraid, angry or really happy. The experience of reading or listening to a story is likely to make us 'feel' that we are part of the story, too. Just like in our 'real' lives, we might love or hate different characters. Perhaps we recognise ourselves or other people we know in some of the story characters. Perhaps they have similar talents, ambitions, weaknesses or problems.

Because of this natural connection with story characters, our brains process the reading of stories differently from the way we read factual information. This is because our brains don't always recognise the difference between an imagined situation and a real one so the characters become 'alive' to us. What they say or do is therefore much more meaningful. The words and structures that relate a story's events, descriptions and conversations are processed by learners in a deeper way.

Encouraging learners to read or listen to stories should therefore help them to learn a second language in a way that is not only fun, but memorable.

How else do stories help?

Stories don't only offer the young reader a chance to learn more vocabulary and develop their grammatical skills. The experience also creates an opportunity to develop critical and creative thinking, emotional literacy and social skills. As learners read a story, they will be imagining far more details than its words communicate. Each learner will, subconsciously, be 'animating' the characters and making judgements and predictions about events.

As a teacher, you can encourage creativity and critical thinking by asking learners in groups to develop characters in more detail, talk about the part of the story they enjoyed most/least or even write different endings. You can also discuss, in English or L1 if necessary, the story 'values', in other words, what different stories teach us about how to relate to others.

Stories also offer a forum for personalised learning. No two learners will feel exactly the same about a story and an acceptance of difference can also be interesting to explore and discuss in class.

How can we encourage learners to join in and ask parents to help?

If, at first, learners lack confidence or motivation to read stories in English, help by reading the story to them without stopping so learners are just enjoying the story, stress free, and following as well as they can by looking at the pictures. During a second reading you might encourage interaction by asking questions like *Is this funny, scary or sad?* (Starters) *Was that a good idea?* (Movers) *What do you think will happen next?* (Flyers). If the class is read to in a relaxed and fun way, learners will subconsciously relate to the reading and language learning process more confidently and positively. Of course, being read to by a parent at home, too, is also simply a lovely way to share quiet and close time. To engage parents in the language learning process, you might share some of the above points with them or encourage them to search online for language learning activities to do at home with their children.

The Home FUN booklet has been specially designed for learners to use at home with parents. Activities are fun and easy to follow, requiring little instruction. The booklet aims to help learners show parents what they have learnt at school and to engage them in the learning process.

Further suggestions for storytelling

- Involve learners in the topic and ask guessing and prediction questions in L1 if necessary. This will engage learners in the process of storytelling and motivate learning. When you pause the audio during the story, ask learners …
  - about the topic and themselves
  - to guess aspects of the story
  - to say how they think a character feels or what they may say next
- If you are telling the story yourself, support your learners in any way you can by adding your own dramatisation. For instance, you can read the stories with as much animation as possible and use props such as puppets or soft toys and different voices to bring the stories to life.
- Incorporate the use of realia into the storytelling process. For example, if you are using *Storyfun 4*, in 'Jane's clever idea' you could bring in the different items that Jane swaps, and in 'The tomango tree' you could bring different fruits into the classroom for learners to taste.
- Once learners are familiar with the story they could even act out parts of the story in role plays. This will not only involve learners in the stories and add a fun element but can also help in practising and consolidating language.

Suggestions for using the story pictures

For skills practice

- Before listening to the story, learners look at all the pictures on the story pages and discuss in small groups who or what they think the story is about and what the key events are.
- Learners trace a picture (adding their own choice of extra details) and then follow your colouring or drawing instructions.

To encourage creative thinking

- Groups choose two people in a picture and imagine what they are saying to each other. They then write a question with answer or a short dialogue.
- Groups choose a background person in a picture and invent details about him/her. For example, how old they are, what they like doing, where they live, what pet they have.
- Groups invent details that are unseen in the picture, for example, ten things in a bag, cupboard or garden.
- Learners imagine they are 'in' the picture. What is behind / in front of / next to them? What can they feel (the sun, a cold wind …), smell (flowers, cooking …) or hear (birds, traffic …)?

To revise vocabulary and grammar

- Learners find as many things in a picture as they can which begin with a particular letter, for example, *f*.
- Learners list things in a picture that are a certain colour or in a certain place. For example, what someone is wearing or what is on the table.
- Learners choose four things they can see in a picture and list the words according to the size of the object or length of the word. Learners could also choose things according to categories such as food or animals.
- Using the pictures to revise grammar, for example *This is / These are*.
- Choose a picture in the story and ask learners in groups to say what is happening in this part of the story.
- Practise prepositions by asking learners what they can see in a picture in different places, for example, in the box, on the table or under the tree.
- Practise question forms by asking learners about different aspects of a picture, for example: *What colour is the cat? How many ducks are there? What's the boy doing?*
- On the board, write the first and last letter of four things learners can remember in a particular story picture. Learners complete the words.
- Point to objects or people in a picture and ask *This/These yes/no* questions. For example: *Is this a shoe? Are these toys? Is this a boy? Are these hats?*
- Ask *yes/no* colour and *how many* questions. For example, point to an apple and ask *Is this apple blue? Can you see four apples?*
- Show learners a story picture for 30 seconds and then ask *What's in that picture?* Write learners' answers on the board.
- Ask simple *What's the word* questions and build on known vocabulary sets. For example: *It's green. You can eat it. It's a fruit.* (a pear / an apple / a grape / a kiwi)

Suggestions for using the word list

At the back of the Student's Book, learners will find a list of important Movers words that appear in each unit.

- Play 'Which word am I?' Learners work in pairs, looking at the word list for the unit. Choose a noun and give the class clues about it until one pair guesses it. Don't make the clues too easy and focus on form first and meaning afterwards. Say, for example: *I've got four letters. The letter 'k' is in me. You can sit on me. You can ride me to school.* (bike)
- Divide the class into A and B pairs. Learner A sits facing the board. Learner B sits with his/her back to the board. Write four words (nouns or verbs are best) from the word list for the unit on the board. Learner A then draws or mimes them until their partner guesses them all and writes them correctly (with the help of Learner A who can only say *Yes, that's right!* or *No, that's wrong!*). When everyone has finished, learners change places. Write some new words on the board. Learner B in each pair mimes these words for Learner A to guess.
- Play 'Tell me more, please!' Choose a noun from the word list for the unit and write it on the board, for example: *banana*. Learners take turns to add more information about the banana. For example, Learner A says: *The banana is long.* Learner B adds: *The banana is long. It's yellow.* Learner C says: *The banana is long. It's yellow. It's a fruit.* Continue until learners can't remember previous information.
- Pairs work together to make as many words from the word list for the unit as they can, using a number of letters that you dictate to the class. Alternatively, use word tiles from board games or letter cards made by the class. These could also be used for spelling tests in pairs or groups.
- On the board, write eight words from the word list for the unit with the letters jumbled. Pairs work as fast as they can to find the words and spell them correctly.
- On the board, write eight words from the word list for the unit. Spell three or four of them incorrectly. Pairs work as fast as they can to identify the misspelt words (they shouldn't be told how many there are) and to write them down correctly.
- Play 'Make a word'. Each group chooses a word (four, five or six letters long) from the word list for the unit and creates it by forming a human sculpture, i.e. learners in each group stand in a line, using their arms or legs to create the shapes of each letter. Remember you may need two learners for some letters (e.g. *k*). When all the groups are ready, the words are guessed.
- Use the word list for the unit to play common word games such as hangman, bingo and definition games or for dictated spelling tests. A nice alternative to the traditional hangman, which learners may enjoy, is an animal with its mouth open, with 8–10 steps leading down into its mouth. (You could use a crocodile at Starters, a shark at Movers or a dinosaur at Flyers.) With each incorrect guess, the stick person falls down onto the next step, and gets eaten if they reach the animal's mouth!

For more information on Cambridge English: Young Learners, please visit. From here, you can download the handbook for teachers, which includes information about each level of the Young Learners tests. You can also find information for candidates and their parents, including links to videos of the Speaking test at each level. There are also sample test papers, as well as further games and songs and links to the Teaching Support website.

A few final classroom points

Please try to be as encouraging as possible when working through the activities. By using phrases such as *Now you! You choose! Well done! Don't worry!* you are also helping learners to feel more confident about participating fully in the class and trying hard to do their best. Make sure that everyone in your class adds to open class work, however minimally, and when mistakes are made, view them as opportunities for learning. Try not to interrupt to correct learners during open class discussion, role plays, etc. Doing so might negatively affect a child's willingness to contribute in future. It takes courage to speak out in class. Make mental notes of mistakes and then cover them at a later moment with the whole class.

Have fun!

But most of all, please remember that an hour's lesson can feel very much longer than that to a learner who feels excluded, fearful of making mistakes, unsure about what to do, unable to follow instructions or express any personal opinions. An hour's lesson will feel like five minutes if a learner is having fun, sensing their own progress and participating fully in enjoyable and meaningful activities.

How is the Student's Book organised?

Story

Four illustrated story pages using language (topics, vocabulary and grammar) needed for the Cambridge English: Movers test.

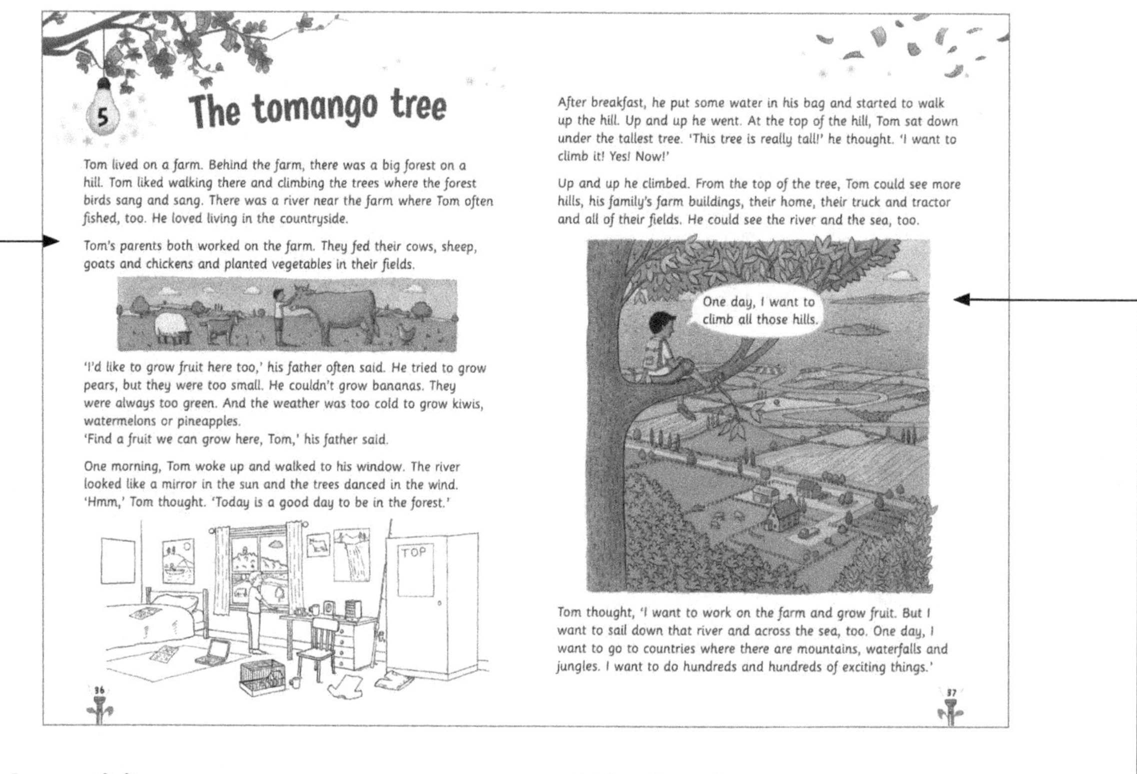

5

The tomango tree

Tom lived on a farm. Behind the farm, there was a big forest on a hill. Tom liked walking there and climbing the trees where the forest birds sang and sang. There was a river near the farm where Tom often fished, too. He loved living in the countryside.

Tom's parents both worked on the farm. They fed their cows, sheep, goats and chickens and planted vegetables in their fields.

'I'd like to grow fruit here too,' his father often said. He tried to grow pears, but they were too small. He couldn't grow bananas. They were always too green. And the weather was too cold to grow kiwis, watermelons or pineapples.
'Find a fruit we can grow here, Tom,' his father said.

One morning, Tom woke up and walked to his window. The river looked like a mirror in the sun and the trees danced in the wind. 'Hmm,' Tom thought. 'Today is a good day to be in the forest.'

After breakfast, he put some water in his bag and started to walk up the hill. Up and up he went. At the top of the hill, Tom sat down under the tallest tree. 'This tree is really tall!' he thought. 'I want to climb it! Yes! Now!'

Up and up he climbed. From the top of the tree, Tom could see more hills, his family's farm buildings, their home, their truck and tractor and all of their fields. He could see the river and the sea, too.

Tom thought, 'I want to work on the farm and grow fruit. But I want to sail down that river and across the sea, too. One day, I want to go to countries where there are mountains, waterfalls and jungles. I want to do hundreds and hundreds of exciting things.'

36 37

Vocabulary activity

Each unit of four-page activities opens with a vocabulary comprehension activity related to the key Cambridge English: Movers vocabulary presented in the story.

Value key phrase

A key English phrase within the story demonstrates the story 'value'. For example, Having a dream for the future ➜ "One day, I want to ..."

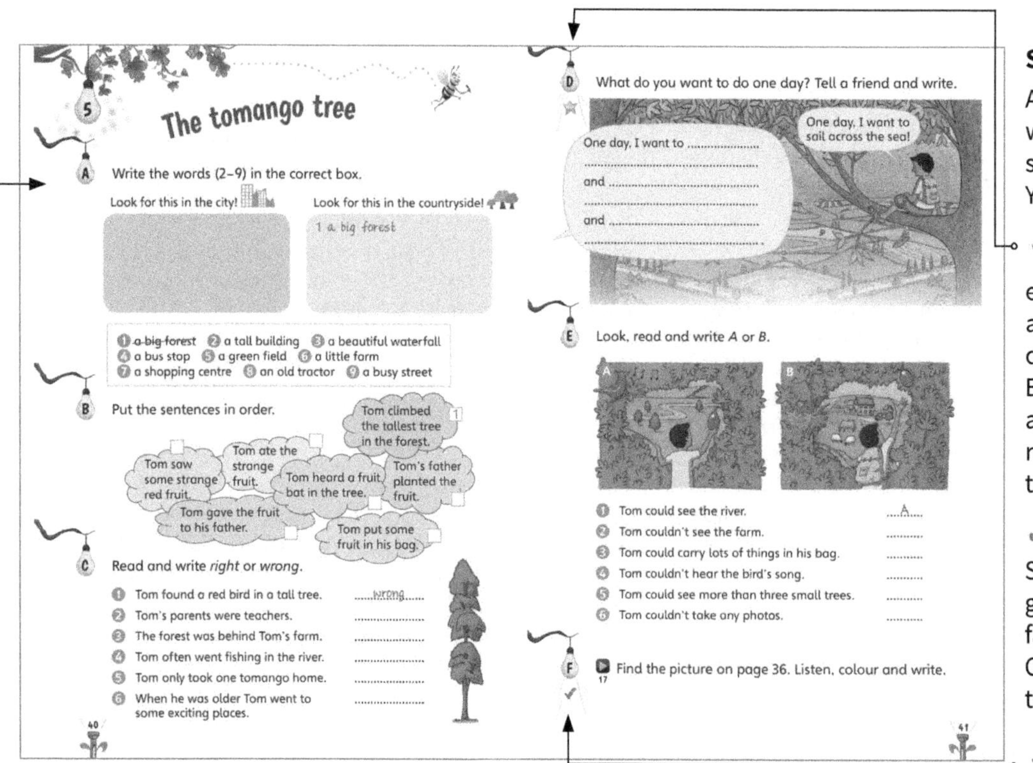

5

The tomango tree

A Write the words (2–9) in the correct box.

Look for this in the city! Look for this in the countryside!

1 a big forest

1 ~~a big forest~~ 2 a tall building 3 a beautiful waterfall 4 a bus stop 5 a green field 6 a little farm 7 a shopping centre 8 an old tractor 9 a busy street

B Put the sentences in order.

Tom climbed the tallest tree in the forest. 1
Tom saw some strange red fruit.
Tom ate the strange fruit.
Tom heard a fruit bat in the tree.
Tom's father planted the fruit.
Tom gave the fruit to his father.
Tom put some fruit in his bag.

C Read and write *right* or *wrong*.

1 Tom found a red bird in a tall tree. ......wrong......
2 Tom's parents were teachers. ....
3 The forest was behind Tom's farm. ....
4 Tom often went fishing in the river. ....
5 Tom only took one tomango home. ....
6 When he was older Tom went to some exciting places. ....

40

D What do you want to do one day? Tell a friend and write.

One day, I want to ....
....
and ....
....
and ....
....

E Look, read and write *A* or *B*.

1 Tom could see the river. ....A....
2 Tom couldn't see the farm. ....
3 Tom could carry lots of things in his bag. ....
4 Tom couldn't hear the bird's song. ....
5 Tom could see more than three small trees. ....
6 Tom couldn't take any photos. ....

F 17 Find the picture on page 36. Listen, colour and write.

41

Skills

All activities develop reading, writing, listening and speaking skills that are useful for the YLE tests.

Value activities

encourage learners to think about the story in a social context and practise the key English phrase. The phrase aids learners to contextualise, remember and demonstrate the value of English.

➜ Practice for Movers

Specific activities that gently build up learners' familiarity and practise for the Cambridge English: Movers test.

✓ Test tasks for Movers

Authentic activities that follow the exact format of Cambridge English: Movers test tasks.

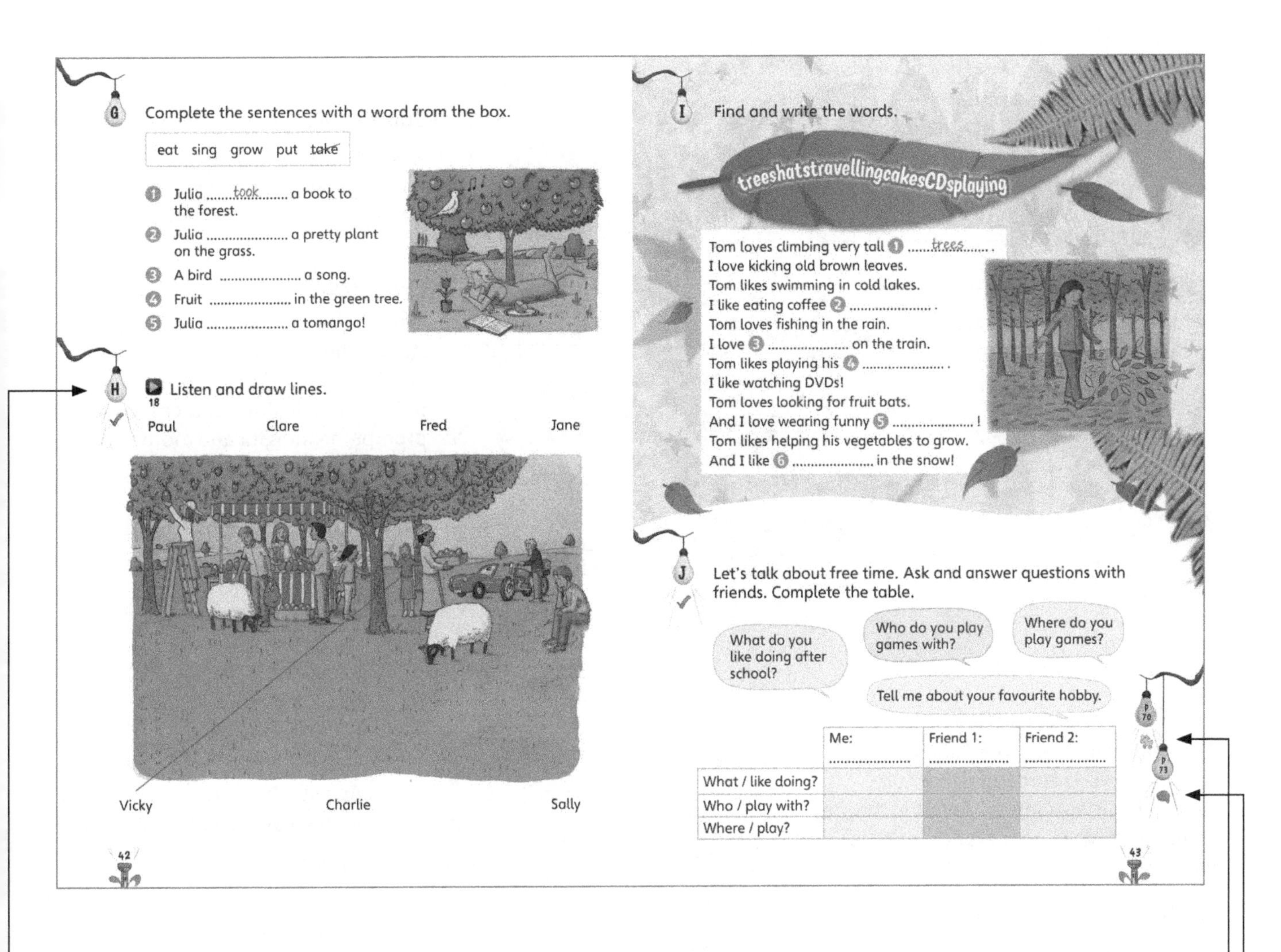

G Complete the sentences with a word from the box.

eat sing grow put ~~take~~

1. Julia ....took.... a book to the forest.
2. Julia .... a pretty plant on the grass.
3. A bird .... a song.
4. Fruit .... in the green tree.
5. Julia .... a tomango!

H Listen and draw lines. 18

Paul Clare Fred Jane

Vicky Charlie Sally

42

I Find and write the words.

treeshatstravellingcakesCDsplaying

Tom loves climbing very tall 1 ....trees.... .
I love kicking old brown leaves.
Tom likes swimming in cold lakes.
I like eating coffee 2 ....
Tom loves fishing in the rain.
I love 3 .... on the train.
Tom likes playing his 4 ....
I like watching DVDs!
Tom loves looking for fruit bats.
And I love wearing funny 5 .... !
Tom likes helping his vegetables to grow.
And I like 6 .... in the snow!

J Let's talk about free time. Ask and answer questions with friends. Complete the table.

What do you like doing after school?
Who do you play games with?
Where do you play games?
Tell me about your favourite hobby.

	Me:	Friend 1:	Friend 2: ....
What / like doing?			
Who / play with?			
Where / play?			

P 70
P 73

43

Accompanying audio tracks can be found on Presentation plus or online

Let's say!

Optional pronunciation practice at the back of the Student's Book focuses on initial key sounds to develop early speaking skills. Supported by accompanying audio.

Let's have fun!

Optional projects or games at the back of the Student's Book to promote collaborative learning.

Let's speak!

Optional extra speaking practice at the back of the Student's Book allows learners to practise the language needed for the speaking part of the Cambridge English: Movers test.

Songs

Open activities such as poems and songs maintain learners' motivation and interest.

How could teachers use *Storyfun 4*?

1. Encourage learners to predict the general topic of the story using flashcards and the story pictures.
2. Teach or revise any Cambridge English: Movers words that are important in the story.
3. Play the audio or read the story.
4. (Optional) Discuss the story 'value' with learners. You will probably need to do this in your learners' first language to fully explore what the story teaches the reader.
5. Present the vocabulary and general comprehension tasks (usually Activities A–C).
6. Present the grammar, vocabulary and skills sections (generally Activities D–H).
7. Encourage collaborative learning with the *Let's have fun!* at the back of the Student's Book.
8. Follow communicative pair- or group-work suggestions in the *Let's speak!* pages at the back of the Student's Book.
9. Use extension activities in the Teacher's Books or set homework tasks.

How is the Teacher's Book organised?

Main topics and grammar
Cambridge English: Movers topics and grammar focused on in the activities in this unit.

Story summary

Main vocabulary
Cambridge English: Movers vocabulary focused on in the activities in this unit.

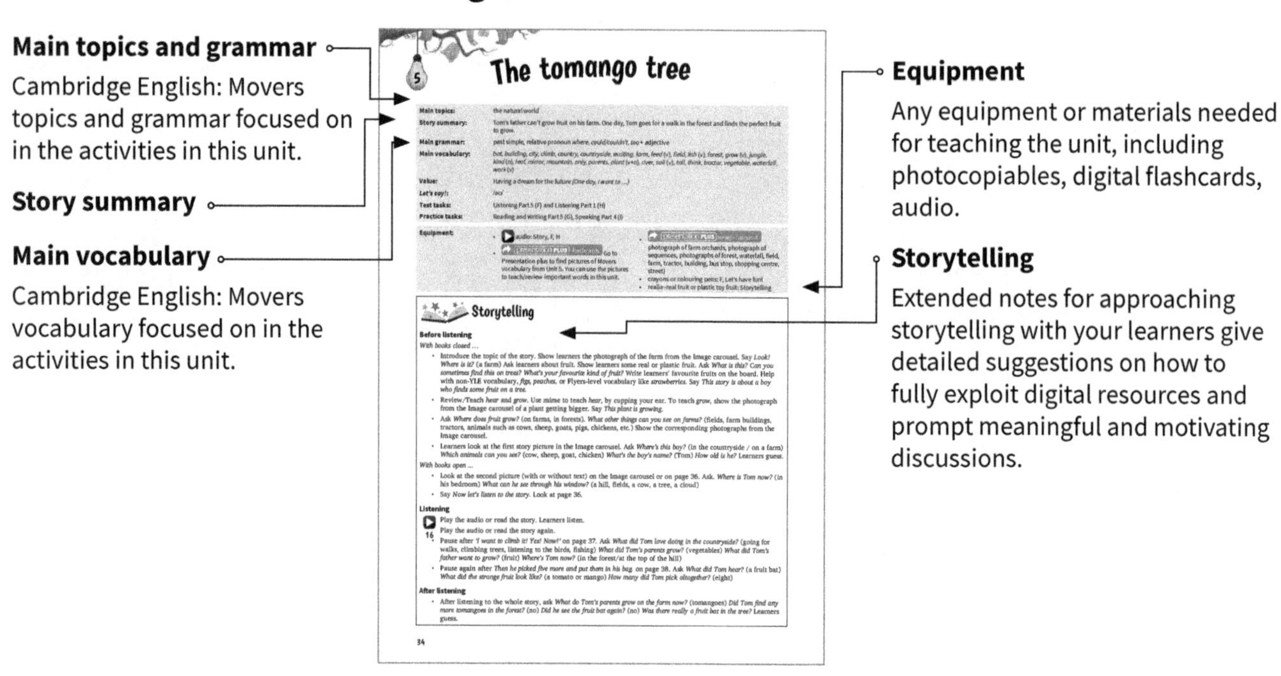

Equipment
Any equipment or materials needed for teaching the unit, including photocopiables, digital flashcards, audio.

Storytelling
Extended notes for approaching storytelling with your learners give detailed suggestions on how to fully exploit digital resources and prompt meaningful and motivating discussions.

Value
The value can be explored and discussed with learners after reading the story. Discussion is optional, either directly after listening or when learners attempt the value activity.

Test tasks for Movers
Authentic activities that follow the exact format of Cambridge English: Movers test tasks.

Practice for Movers
Specific activities that gently build up learners' familiarity and practise for the Cambridge English: Movers test.

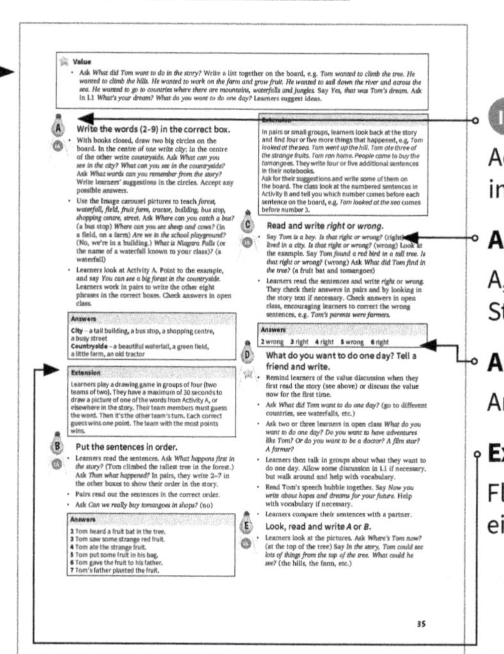

Interactive activity
Activity that can also be completed interactively on Presentation plus.

Activity notes
A, B, C, etc. sections correspond to Student's Book activities.

Answer keys
Answers or suggested answers.

Extension activities
Flexible ideas to extend activities either in class or for homework.

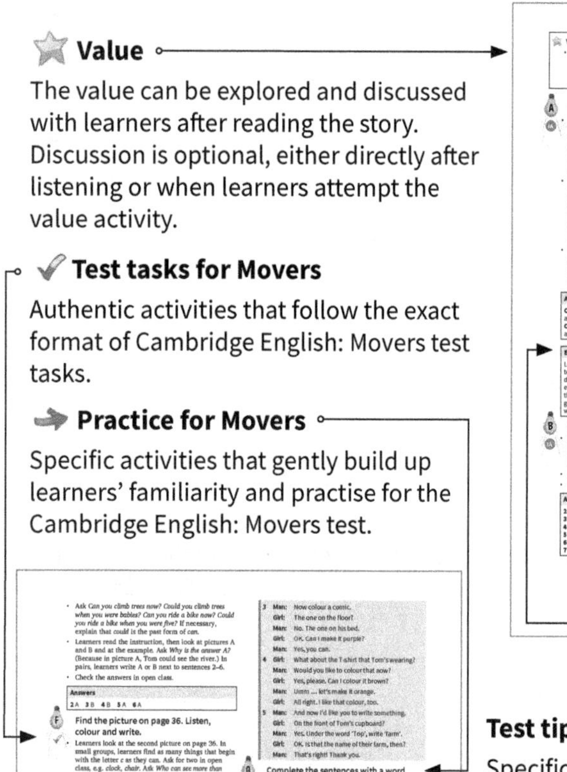

Test tips and practice
Specific tips for the Cambridge English: Movers test with optional accompanying activity.

Audio
Track listing for accompanying audio on Presentation plus, or online

Audioscripts
All scripts for listening activities in the Student's Book. Scripts for stories are not listed.

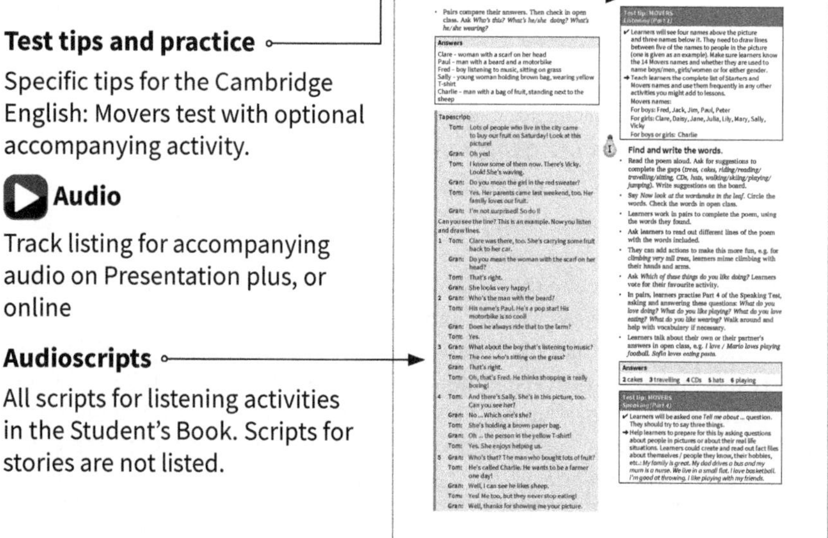

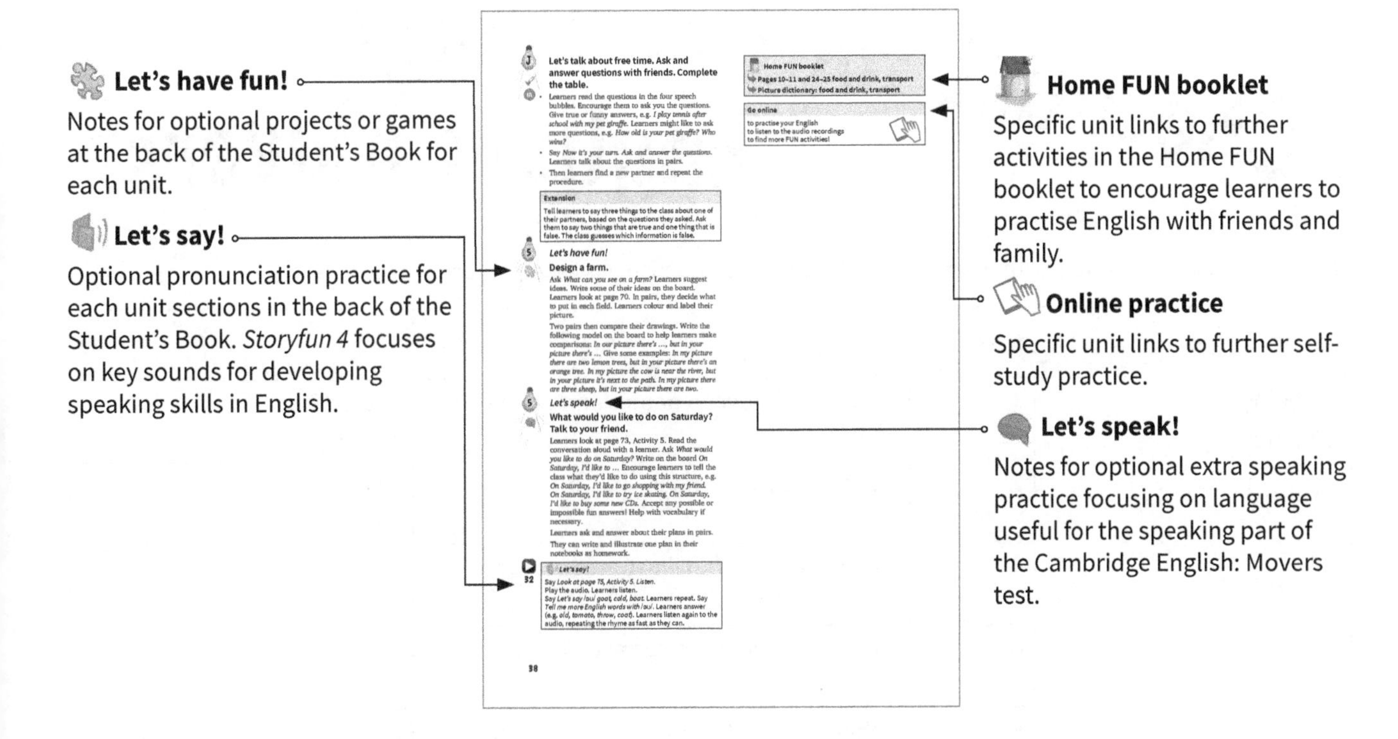

How is the digital organised?

Presentation plus

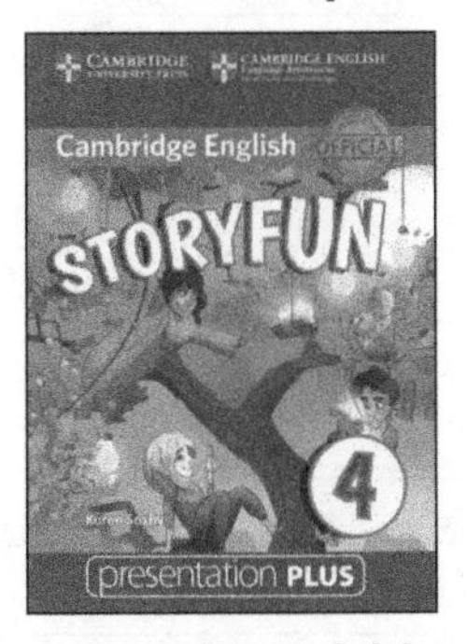

Interactive activities

Every 'Activity A' in each unit is interactive to check vocabulary comprehension after reading the story and encourage whole-class participation. Other IA activities can be used as a supporting feature, either as a means of introducing an activity, scaffolding, or during answer feedback.

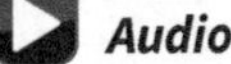

Audio

All audio can be launched from the audio icon. Accompanying audioscripts can be displayed on screen.

Answer key

All activities have a visual answer key to easily display and check answers with your learners.

Digital flashcards

All Cambridge English: Movers test words are supported with visual flashcards with accompanying audio.

Image carousel

These additional images can be used to prompt further discussion on themes and concepts. Ideas of when and how to use them are within the teacher's notes for each unit.

Each story also has a collection of separate images of the Student's Book pictures without text to prompt discussion before learners open their books and listen, revise the story if heard in a previous lesson or to use as a wrapping-up activity where learners can re-tell the story they've listened to.

Online practice

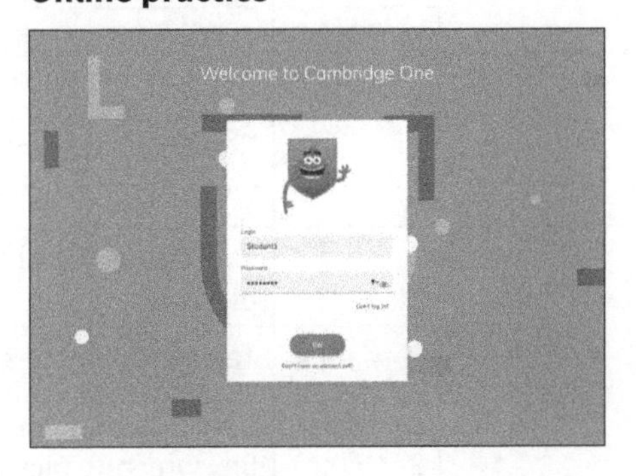

For the Teacher

- Presentation plus
- All audio recordings
- Additional digital resources to support your classes

For the Student

- Fun activities to practise the exam, skills and language
- All audio recordings
- Additional digital resources

Word FUN World app

Checklist for Cambridge English: Movers

Storyfun 4 provides learners with examples of all Cambridge English: Movers test tasks.

Paper	Part	Task	Unit
Listening 25 minutes	**1**	Draw lines between names and people in a picture.	Practice: 8 Test: 5
	2	Write words or numbers in a form.	Practice: 7, 8 Test: 3
	3	Match pictures with illustrated words.	Test: 1
	4	Tick boxes under the correct picture.	Practice: 6 Test: 4
	5	Colour different parts of a picture and write.	Practice: 2, 3 Test: 5
Reading and Writing 30 minutes	**1**	Copy correct words next to definitions.	Practice: 1, 4, 6, 8 Test: 2
	2	Choose correct response by circling a letter.	Test: 1
	3	Choose and copy missing words into a story text.	Practice: 3 Test: 4
	4	Complete a text by copying the correct grammatical words.	Test: 8
	5	Complete sentences about a story by writing one, two or three words.	Practice: 5 Test: 7
	6	Complete sentences, answer questions and write two sentences about a picture.	Practice: 3, 4, 8 Test: 6, 7
Speaking 5–7 minutes	**1**	Talk about the differences between two pictures.	Test: 1, 6
	2	Tell a story by describing pictures.	Practice: 7 Test: 2
	3	Say why one picture is different from three others in a set.	Test: 3
	4	Answer personal questions.	Test: 5, 8

Map of the Student's Book

Story and Unit	Value	Topics	Grammar	Test tasks for Movers
1 Jane's clever idea	Creative thinking (*"Would you like ...? I'd like ..."*)	friends possessions hobbies	*would you like, I'd like/love* irregular past simple forms *I need* *I like ... more than ...*	Reading and Writing Part 2 Listening Part 3 Speaking Part 1
2 The perfect present	Appreciation of nature and people (*"It's so beautiful here."*)	nature school	relative clauses with *that* comparative adjectives: *nicer, more beautiful*	Reading and Writing Part 1 Speaking Part 2
3 Daisy's tiger dream	Being a good friend (*"I can be a good friend."*)	home animals the natural world	comparative adjectives *can* *could/couldn't* *be good at*	Listening Part 2 Speaking Part 3
4 A busy Monday	Being productive (*"I like being busy!"*)	home activities at home	*must* simple past regular and irregular *How about ...?*	Reading and Writing Part 3 Listening Part 4
5 The tomango tree	Having a dream for the future (*"One day, I want to ..."*)	the natural world	past simple relative pronoun *where* *could/couldn't* *too* + adjective	Listening Parts 1 and 5 Speaking Part 4
6 Do whales have stomach-ache?	Wanting to learn about the world (*"Do you know ...?"*)	health parts of the body animals	superlative adjectives *have to* *must*	Reading and Writing Part 6 Speaking Part 1
7 The grey cloud	Making others feel happier (*"That's better!"*)	nature feelings weather	comparative adverbs and adjectives: *bad, worse, worst; good, better, best*	Reading and Writing Parts 5 and 6
8 The fancy-dress shop	Saying how you feel (*"This is getting scary!"*)	clothes jobs feelings	*How about ...?* *What about ...?*	Reading and Writing Part 4 Speaking Part 4

1 Jane's clever idea

Main topics:	friends, possessions and hobbies
Story summary:	Jane loves riding her bike, but she needs a new wheel. She has an idea to get one.
Main grammar:	*would you like, I'd like/love,* irregular past simple forms, *I need, I like … more than …*
Main vocabulary:	*around, band, CD, cool, fantastic, fix* (v), *front, go for a walk, ground, helmet, ice skates, lake, laptop, laugh, need* (v), *outside, park, present, quickly, rabbit, ride, skateboard, slow, sorry, swimsuit, tennis racket, think, times, wheel*
Value:	Creative thinking (*"Would you like … ?" "I'd like …"*)
***Let's say!*:**	/w/
Practice tasks:	Reading and Writing Part 1 (A)
Test tasks:	Reading and Writing Part 2 (D), Listening Part 3 (F), Speaking Part 1 (H)

Equipment:

- audio: Story, F, I
- presentation PLUS flashcards
  Go to Presentation plus to find pictures of Movers vocabulary from Unit 1. You can use the pictures to teach/review important words in this unit.
- presentation PLUS Image carousel 1–6
  (Italian lake town, fruit, vegetables, cycling, skateboarding, playing tennis): Storytelling, E
- Photocopy 1 (TB page 54) (one per learner): Let's have fun!
- wooden sticks and glue/tape: Let's have fun!
- crayons / colouring pencils: E Extension

Storytelling

Before listening

With books closed …

- Introduce the topic of the story. Ask *What are your favourite sports or hobbies?* Write five or six suggestions on the board. Learners vote for the most interesting hobby. Review/Teach *tennis racket, swimsuit, CDs*. Say *This story is about a girl who loves riding her bike.*
- Show learners the picture of the town by the lake from the Image carousel. Say *Look! Where is it?* (a town near a lake) *Let's read a story about this place.*
- Look at the first two story pictures (with or without the text) on the Image carousel or on page 4. Point to the bike. Say *Jane loves riding her bike. Do you have a bike? Where do you like riding it?* Teach *wheel* by pointing to the wheel on the bike. Next, learners look at the first picture. Ask *Where is this girl?* (near a lake) *What's she wearing?* (glasses, shorts, T-shirt) Review/Teach *helmet.* Ask *How old is she?* Learners guess.
- Say *Now let's listen to the story. Look at page 4.*

Listening

With books open …

02

- Play the audio or read the story. Learners listen.
- Play the audio or read the story again.
- Pause after *'You can walk to school and the shops and go for nice walks in the park, Jane,' her mother answered.* on page 5. Ask *Why did Jane stop quickly?* (Because a rabbit hopped out in front of her.) *Can Jane's mum buy her a new wheel?* (no) *Why not?* (She needs to buy a swimsuit for Jane's sister and a present for Jane's grandmother.) *Does Jane want to walk to school and the shops and in the park?* (no) *What can she do?* Learners suggest ideas, in L1 if necessary.
- Pause again after *Then Jane went to find her friend Matt.* on page 5.
- Ask *Has Sam got a wheel for Jane's bike?* (no) *What has she got?* (a tennis racket) *Which does Jane like better, her ice skates or Sam's tennis racket?* (Sam's tennis racket) *What do they do?* (Jane gives Sam her ice skates and Sam gives Jane her tennis racket.) Teach *swap*: mime swapping pens or pencils with a student so learners understand the idea that the characters in the story are exchanging items.
- Listen to the whole story, then ask *What did Matt give Jane for the tennis racket?* (five CDs) *What did Paul give Jane for the CDs?* (a skateboard) *Who liked the skateboard?* (Clare) *What did Clare give Jane?* (her old bike)

After listening

- Ask *Is Jane happy at the end of the story?* (yes) *Why?* (She's got two new wheels for her bike.) *What did she need?* (one new wheel) Say *Look at the name of the story. What is Jane's clever idea?* (swapping things with her friends to get what she needs) Accept answers in L1 if necessary.

Value

- Say *Look at pages 6 and 7.* Ask *What objects do the friends swap? How are they creative? Why is Jane's idea a creative idea?* Learners say why in L1.
- Ask *Do you swap objects with your friends? What creative ideas do you have when you need something?* (e.g. ask your parents, ask your friends, make it, save money for it, etc.)

A Read and draw lines.

- Ask learners to cover the answers in Activity A with a book or a piece of paper. Read the definitions together and ask learners to suggest possible answers. Accept any possible answers. Then say *Now look at the answers.* Read the example together. In pairs, learners draw lines from the words to the correct definitions.

Answers
2 a swimsuit **3** presents **4** a helmet **5** CDs **6** a pair

Extension

Write the following words from the story on the board:
skateboard, lake, bedroom, kitchen, park, shops, ice skates, tennis racket, bike
Write these structures on the board:
You can ________________ *here.*
You use this/these to ________________.
Ask *What can you do in a lake?* (swim) Say *Write sentences to describe the words*, e.g. *You can sleep here.* (a bedroom) *You can buy things here.* (shop(s)) *You can use this to play tennis.* (a (tennis) racket) Walk around and help learners write their definitions. Put learners in pairs. One learner reads a sentence and the other guesses the word.

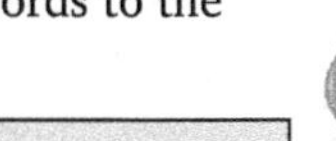

Test tip: MOVERS
Reading and Writing (Part 1)

✔ The answers, e.g. *a blanket*, that learners have to write are shown under the pictures. Learners should make sure they copy the words carefully because they must be spelled correctly.

➜ When practising this task, tell learners to check they have copied each of their answers correctly and ask *How many letters are there in (e.g.) 'skateboard'?* In any lesson, write key or interesting words on the board and tell learners to copy them into their vocabulary books.

B Put the sentences in order.

- Ask *What happened at the start of the story?* (Jane fell off her bike.) *What happened at the end of the story?* (Jane got another bike from Clare.) Learners look at Activity B. Ask *What happened first?* (Jane saw a rabbit on the path.) Say *Look at the letter h. Look at the number 1 in the blue shape. Now put the story in order. Write the numbers.*
- Learners work in pairs to order the sentences, checking against the story if they need to. When they finish, learners check with another pair before checking in open class. Practise ordinal numbers and ask *What happened first? What happened second?*

Answers
a 5 **b** 4 **c** 2 **d** 6 **e** 8 **f** 7 **g** 3

C What might Jane say? Tick (✔) the correct answer.

- In L1, ask *What do you think the story teaches us?* Accept all valid answers. Say *Read the sentences in Activity C.* Ask *Which of these does the story teach us?* Learners work in pairs and choose the best answer.
- Ask learners to say all the things they can reuse by giving them to their friends, or younger brothers, sisters or cousins, e.g. clothes, toys. Ask *What toys have you got which you never use? Who can you give them to?*

Answers
C You don't always need to buy new things.

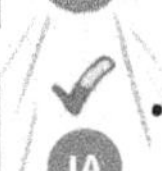

D Read the text and choose the best answer.

- Learners look at the picture in Activity D. Ask *Who can you see?* (Jane and a boy) Say *The boy's called Ben. Where are they?* (at the lake) *What are they doing?* (talking, cycling around the lake)
- Read the example together. Say *Ben and Jane are talking. Which is the correct answer?* (C) Ask in L1 *How do you know?* (Ben asks where, and answer C is a place.)
- Learners work in pairs and choose the best answers.
- Check answers in open class. Ask pairs to role play the conversations with the correct answers included.

Answers
1 B **2** A **3** C **4** B **5** A

Extension

Pairs practise the mini-conversations together with the original answers. Pairs then role play the conversations again and add more information to the answer. Brainstorm ideas with the class first, e.g:
I love riding my bike here!
So do I! This lake is brilliant/cool/fantastic!

Cool helmet! Is it new?
No, it was my cousin's.
It's great/cool/brilliant! My helmet is old/new/green/etc.

And what's in your bag?
A bottle of water and a map / a pencil / an orange / my homework / etc.

Encourage learners to practise the conversations without reading the sentences. Learners act out some of their conversations for the class.

What do you like? Look and say with *more* and *the most*.

- Use photographs of sets of related items from the Image carousel to ask learners to make comparisons. Model the structure for learners to repeat: *I like vegetables, but I like* (fruit) *more. I like* (bananas) *the most! What about you? I like riding my bike, but I like* (skateboarding) *more. I like playing* (tennis) *the most. And you?*
- Write the model on the board:
  I like ____________ *, but I like* ____________ *more.*
  I like ____________ *the most!*
  Learners look at the pictures in Activity E and use the model to make sentences.
- Ask learners about their friend: *What does* (Ruben) *like doing most? What animal does* (Agata) *like most?*

Extension

Learners draw pairs of pictures to continue the speaking activity. Ask them to draw two fruits, two animals and two activities. Then they make sentences about them in pairs, using *more* and *the most.*

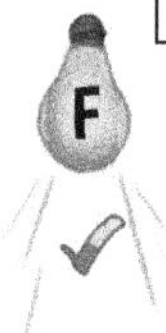

Mr Pool is telling Jane about the people in his family. What does each person really like doing? Listen and write a letter in each box.

- Say *My sister likes playing basketball.* Ask *What do people in your family like doing?*
- Learners look at the pictures. Say *This is Mr Pool's family. Can you see his son?* Learners point. *Can you see his daughter? Where's his granddaughter?* Now point to their hobbies. Ask *What do the people in Mr Pool's family like doing? Who enjoys cooking? Who enjoys listening to music?* Learners guess.

- Say *Now listen to Mr Pool. He's talking to Jane.* Play the audio, pausing after the example. Say *What does Mr Pool's grandson enjoy playing?* (baseball) *Look at the letter G. Now you write the letters.* Play the rest of the audio.

Answers

cousin D daughter E granddaughter C son B
father A

Tapescript:

Man:	Hi, Jane. Wow! Great bike!
Jane:	Thanks, Mr Pool.
Man:	My grandson's too young to ride a bike, but he loves baseball!
Jane:	Really! That's fantastic. Me too!

Can you see the letter G? Now you listen and write a letter in each box.

Man:	My daughter's a very busy person.
Jane:	Yes, I saw her in town yesterday. She likes buying things, I think!
Man:	That's right! Her favourite place is the new shopping centre!
Jane:	Really! I don't like going there!
Man:	I've got a granddaughter, too!
Jane:	I didn't know that!
Man:	She's only little, but she really enjoys listening to pop music!
Jane:	Wow! So do I!
Man:	My son isn't working today. He's at the park.
Jane:	What's he doing there?
Man:	Skateboarding. It's his favourite hobby.
Jane:	But isn't he a grown-up?
Man:	Yes! Some grown-ups enjoy doing that, too, you know!
Man:	When she was younger, my cousin loved ice skating!
Jane:	Does she do that now?
Man:	No, but she goes to a swimming class. She enjoys that a lot.
Jane:	Where does she do that?
Man:	At the sports centre on Sunday evenings.
Man:	My father's 80 today. I gave him a new phone.
Jane:	Wow! Can he send text messages on it?
Man:	He tries, but he makes mistakes!
Jane:	Oh! What does he really like doing?
Man:	He loves cooking. But I have to go now. Bye, Jane.
Jane:	Bye!

Test tip: MOVERS
Listening (Part 3)

✔ Learners hear a conversation between two people and, after looking at an example, have to match a set of five items, e.g. people, objects, clothing, sports, weather conditions, with a choice of seven, e.g. animals, places, hobbies, food, transport. The sets are shown as pictures. In the first set, the word is given.

➜ Family words are sometimes used in the first set. Make sure learners understand all of these at Starters and Movers levels. In any unit, you could ask questions about story characters, e.g. *What's Jane's sister's/aunt's name? Where does her uncle live?* Learners invent answers. Movers family words: *aunt, daughter, granddaughter, grandson, grandparent, parents, son, uncle.*

Read and draw lines.

- Tell learners you have a problem. Say *I have no food in my kitchen. What can I do?* Learners make suggestions, e.g. *Let's go to the shop. You can eat in a restaurant. You can go to your friend's house.*
- Say *Look at these problems.* Point to the left-hand column in Activity G. Ask some learners to read out the problems. Don't read the solutions yet. Say *What can you do?* Learners suggest a few solutions before reading the example. Encourage learners to mime the suggestions. Learners read the second column and draw lines to match the problems and solutions.
- Check the answers. Read the problems. Learners say the solutions.

Answers

2 Well, let's sing a song! **3** Well, we can make some! **4** Well, we can play in my room! **5** Well, let's find a website! **6** Well, let's wash them!

Find five differences. Point and say.

- Learners look at the two pictures. Say *Some things in the two pictures are different. In this picture* (point to the first picture) *it's raining. But in this picture* (point to the second picture) *it's …* (sunny).
- Write this model on the board: *In this picture it's raining, but in this picture it's sunny.* Drill the model in open class.
- Learners work in groups of four and find four other differences and describe them. Help with vocabulary if necessary. Four groups each share one difference with the class.

Answers

First picture	Second picture
It's raining.	It's sunny.
The ducks are in the lake.	The ducks are on the grass.
There is one child.	There are two children.
Someone is fishing in the lake.	No-one is fishing in the lake.
There are two big trees.	There are four big trees.

Extension

Say *Look at the two pictures again.* Learners practise using the pictures to tell a short story (as in Speaking Part 2). In L1, explain that learners should say three or four simple things about each picture.
Suggested story: *Jane's riding her bike. It's raining. There are some ducks in the lake. Jane's with her friend now. It's sunny and the ducks are on the grass!*

Test tip: MOVERS
Speaking (Part 1)

✔ Learners will need to say something about one picture and then say how the second picture is different.
➜ Teach learners a format in which to talk about the differences, e.g. *In this picture (…), but in this picture (…)!*

Listen and sing. Then change the coloured words.

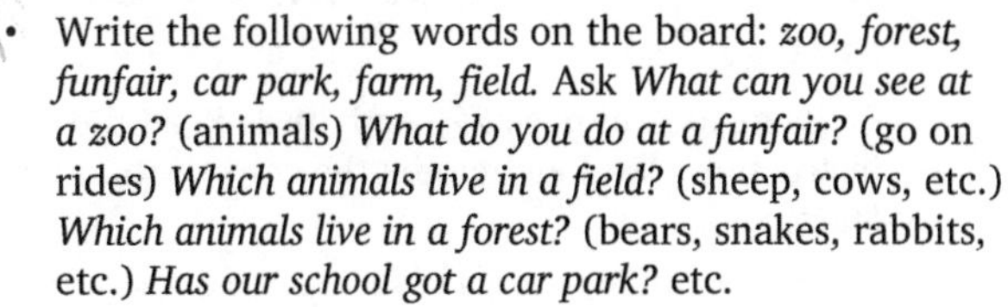

- Write the following words on the board: *zoo, forest, funfair, car park, farm, field.* Ask *What can you see at a zoo?* (animals) *What do you do at a funfair?* (go on rides) *Which animals live in a field?* (sheep, cows, etc.) *Which animals live in a forest?* (bears, snakes, rabbits, etc.) *Has our school got a car park?* etc.

04

- Learners read the coloured words, then close their books. Say *Listen to the song. When you hear the words, stand up.* Play the audio. Learners stand up and sit down as quickly as possible. You can repeat the process, changing the action, e.g. learners raise their hands, high five their friend, etc. when they hear the words.
- Play the audio again. Learners sing the song while reading the words.
- Say *Now let's change the words. I do like to ride my bike up that …* (hill/street/mountain/etc.) Continue to read the song, pausing for learners to suggest different words.
- Learners work in pairs to write their new versions of the song. Help with vocabulary if necessary.

36

- You can also play a version of this song without the words for learners to sing along to.

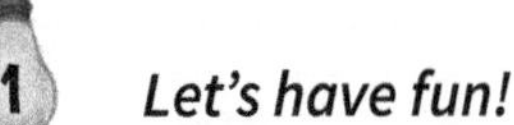

Let's have fun!

Make puppets and act out a story.

Learners look at page 68, Activity 1. Ask *What can you see?* (puppets) *Who are they?* (Jane and her friends)

Give each learner a copy of Photocopy 1 (TB page 54). Tell learners to cut out the characters and objects. Ask them to glue or tape the characters onto sticks. Say *Now tell the story.* In groups of three to four, learners practise telling the story with the character puppets and pointing to the objects at the appropriate times. Walk around as the groups practise phrases and help with vocabulary if necessary.

Groups can perform their 'play' for the rest of the class.

Let's speak!

What do you like to do? Where? Ask and answer.

Learners look at page 72, Activity 1. Read the instruction aloud and model the conversation with a learner.

Ask learners *What do you like to do?* Learners suggest a range of hobbies. *Where do you like reading / swimming / riding your bike?* Learners suggest a range of places. Learners continue the mini-conversation in pairs. Stronger learners can expand it, adding more phrases, such as *Me too! That's nice! What about you?* etc.

Pairs can perform their role plays for the class.

28

Let's say!

Say *Look at page 74, Activity 1. Listen.*
Play the audio. Learners listen.
Say *Let's say /w/ white.* Say *Tell me more English words with /w/.* Learners answer (e.g. *swan, wheel, when, wash, with, water*). Learners listen again to the audio, repeating the rhyme as fast as they can.

Home FUN booklet

Pages 18–19 and 31 sports and leisure, my things

Picture dictionary: sports and leisure

Go online

to practise your English
to listen to the audio recordings
to find more FUN activities!

2 The perfect present

Main topics:	nature, school
Story summary:	Jim wants to get something for his favourite teacher, Miss Point. Mr and Mrs Star and their daughter Grace help him choose the perfect present.
Main grammar:	relative clauses with *that*, comparative adjectives: *nicer, more beautiful*
Main vocabulary:	*all right, angry, basketball, bean, beautiful, bee, bowl, break, butterfly, cheese, choose, circle, classmate, daughter, difficult, duck, earache, email, enough, field, five hundred, fly, forest, frog, grapes, grass, great, idea, internet, leaf/leaves, lime, lizard, mistake, mountain, parrot, pea, perfect, picnic, pretty, river, rock, salad, sand, shape, ship, sky, spelling, trip, try* (v), *watch* (n+v), *weekend, word, work*
Value:	Appreciation of nature and people (*"It's so beautiful here."*)
***Let's say!*:**	/s/
Practice tasks:	Listening Part 5 (H)
Test tasks:	Reading and Writing Part 1 (E), Speaking Part 2 (G)

Equipment:

- audio: Story, H, I
- 

Go to Presentation plus to find pictures of Movers vocabulary from Unit 2. You can use the pictures to teach/review important words in this unit.
- presentation PLUS Image carousel 7–13 (classroom, teacher, five beautiful places): Storytelling, C
- Photocopy 2 (TB page 55) (one per learner): Let's have fun!
- small rectangle of plain paper or card for each learner (A5 size, approximately 148mm x 210 mm): F Extension
- crayons / colouring pencils: F Extension, H, Let's have fun!

Storytelling

Before listening

With books closed …

- Introduce the topic of the story. Show learners the photographs of the classroom and teacher from the Image carousel. Say *Look! Where is it?* (a classroom) *Who works here?* (a teacher) *This is a story about a boy who wants to give his teacher a present.*
- Review/Teach *present.* Ask *Do you like giving presents? Is it easy or difficult to choose presents?* Review/Teach *perfect.* Ask *What is the perfect present to give a teacher?* Write learners' suggestions on the board.
- Look at the first two story pictures (with or without the text) on the Image carousel or on page 12. Ask *Where are these children and their teacher in the first picture?* (at school, in the playground) *What are they playing?* (basketball) Review/Teach *break.* Ask *Is this the morning or afternoon break?* (morning) Point to the second picture. Ask *Where is the boy in the cap now?* (next to a river) *What's he thinking about?* Learners guess.
- Say *Now let's listen to the story. Look at page 12.*

Listening

With books open …

05

- Play the audio or read the story. Learners listen.
- Play the audio or read the story again.
- Pause after *'It's so beautiful here,' Jim said.* on page 12. Ask *Who is Jim's favourite teacher?* (Miss Point) *What does he want to give her?* (a present) *Why?* (She's helped him learn lots of different things.) *Where does he go to think?* (to the river) *Which animals does he see?* (a frog, flies, a lizard, bees, ducks)
- Pause again after *'Yes!' said Jim, 'She likes salad! My aunt grows salad leaves in her garden. I can take her some of those … But that's not enough.'* on page 14. Ask *Who does Jim meet?* (Mr Star, Mrs Star and Grace) *What does Jim say Miss Point likes?* (the internet, trips on the train, weekends) *What colour does she like?* (green)
- Play the rest of the audio. At the end of the story, ask *What does Jim decide to give Miss Point?* (green salad leaves, blue grapes and yellow cheese for a picnic) *Is it a good present?* Learners discuss.

After listening

- Ask *Who do you give presents to? When do you give them presents? What's a perfect present for your teacher?*

Value

- Ask *Where does Jim go to think?* (the river) In L1, ask *Why does this place help Jim to think?* Accept any valid answer e.g. *It's quiet, it's beautiful.*
- Ask *Where do you go to think? Is it a quiet place? Is it a beautiful place? Do you like looking at nature? Which animals do you like watching?*
- Ask *Who helps you with your problems? Who do you want to say thank you to?*

Read and complete the words.

- With books closed, draw a stick man on the board with some waves near him. Write the following on the board: *l _ _ _ _ d.* Say *This is a word from the story. It's an animal. Say the letters to spell the word.* Learners suggest letters, without saying the word. Explain they can only make four mistakes in their letter choice. Every time someone suggests a wrong letter, draw the stick man one step closer to the water. After four wrong letters, draw the man falling in the water. Repeat the game with key words from the story, e.g. *trip, internet, break, mistake, picnic, email,* etc.
- Learners open their books and look at Activity A. Point to the lizard and ask *What's this?* (a lizard) Then look at the example together. Say *Write the letters. Complete the words.* Learners work on their own, then compare answers with a partner. Check answers in open class, correcting pronunciation of letters if necessary.

Answers

2 internet **3** break **4** mistake **5** picnic **6** emails

Read and circle the correct answer.

- Say *Let's remember the story. Jim wanted to buy a present for his …* (teacher) *He went to the …* (river) *He watched a frog, a lizard, some bees and some …* (ducks) *The frog ate some …* (flies) *Then Mr and Mrs Star came with Grace. Grace was their …* (daughter) *They helped Jim choose a …* (present)
- Learners look at the example in Activity B. Ask *What did the frog eat?* (some flies) Say *Look! There's a circle around 'flies'. Now you read and draw circles around the correct words.*
- Learners complete the activity in pairs, looking at the story if they need to. Check answers in open class by asking learners to read the whole sentence.

Answers

2 daughter **3** field **4** aunt **5** grapes **6** sun

Extension

Say *Work in pairs.* Learners write three more sentences about the story. Each sentence has one right and one wrong word in it, as in Activity B. Pairs swap sentences and circle the correct answers.

Look at the picture on page 12 and talk with a friend.

- Remind learners of the value discussion when they first read the story (see above) or discuss the value now for the first time.
- Learners look at the river picture on page 12. Ask *What can you see?* (a boat on a river, a boy sitting beside the river) *What animals can you see?* (ducks, a frog, a lizard, bees) Point to the box of adjectives on page 16 and read the example speech bubble aloud, prompting learners to fill the gap *Wow! The …* (river/flowers is/are) *beautiful.* Say *Now you use the describing words to talk about the picture.*
- Discuss beautiful places learners have visited or know about. Ask *Do you know any really pretty places? Where are they? What is the most beautiful place in your town?* Accept answers in English or L1. You can also use the photographs of beautiful places on the Image carousel as prompts.

Extension

For homework, suggest learners go for a slow walk (real or imagined) with family or friends in a local park. They should think about what they see and hear there. Ask questions for learners to think about, e.g. *How many different kinds of animal can you see? Are the trees all the same or different? What can you hear?* Learners write notes and talk about their walk in the next lesson.

Read and draw lines.

- Draw two ducks on the board. Point to one duck. Write *This is a duck. The duck ate some grass.* Ask *How many sentences are there?* (two) Ask *What did this duck do?* (ate some grass) Now, under that duck, write *This is the duck that ate some grass.* Ask *How many sentences are there?* (one) Next, point to the other duck. Write under that duck *This is a duck. The duck ate some bread.* Ask *How many sentences are there?* (two) Ask *What did this duck do?* (ate some bread) Write under that duck *This is the duck that ate some bread.* Ask *How many sentences are there?* (one) Ask *Which is the duck that ate some grass?* Learners point. *Which is the duck that ate some bread?* Learners point.
- Say *Let's make more sentences with 'that'.* Look at the example for Activity D together, on page 17. Ask *What did Jim do?* (He chose a present for his teacher.) Say *Here's the present that Jim chose for his teacher. Make more sentences. Draw lines.* Explain, in L1 if necessary, that there are two extra endings. In pairs, learners complete the activity. Check answers in open class, asking learners to read the whole sentence.

Answers

2 This is the mountain **that** Jim's parents climbed.
3 There's the frog **that** ate three fat flies.
4 These are the plants **that** we grow in our field.
5 This is the walk **that** we went on last weekend.
6 Those are the bees **that** flew above our blue flowers.

Look and read. Choose the correct words and write them on the lines.

- With books closed, give some definitions of words from the story for learners to guess, e.g. *You can travel in this very fast.* (a train or a plane) *This is a place where cows and sheep live.* (a field) *This is a place with lots of trees.* (a forest)
- Learners look at Activity E. Ask *How many pictures are there?* (eight) *How many sentences are there?* (six (including the example)) Say *There are two extra pictures.* Read the example together. Say *Now you find the correct picture and write the word.* Learners write the words on their own, then compare their answers in pairs.

Answers

1 a salad
2 a snail
3 a picnic
4 homework
5 a parrot

Test tip: MOVERS
Reading and Writing (Part 1)

✔ Learners have to read and understand five definitions/clues and match them to five nouns. Learners should read the definitions carefully. There will only be five correct answers, but there will also be two wrong ones that are similar in some ways to the correct ones!
The nouns may come from two or three different topic sets. Most nouns are singular, but some may be uncountable or plural.

➜ When you are teaching a lexical set, e.g. animals, it is often useful to make links with other animals that are similar in some way. So if you are teaching *rabbit*, you might also teach *kangaroo,* as both these animals hop. If you are teaching *shark*, teach *whale* and *dolphin,* too, as these also live in the sea.

Read the text and then write one from you.

- Point to the first text. Ask *What's this?* (a text message) Say *Imagine you are on holiday and you are writing a message. Who are you writing to?* Learners suggest ideas. *What are you doing on holiday?* Learners suggest ideas for activities. *What's the weather like?* Learners suggest ideas.
- Learners read the text with missing information. In L1 if necessary, ask what kind of information is missing in each gap. Suggestions may include a verb, interesting animals or objects, an adjective to describe the weather, an emotion adjective to describe a person and a day of the week.
- In pairs, learners plan and complete their messages. Then they 'send' it to another pair in the class to read out.

Extension

Give each learner a small rectangular card. Learners answer the top message in Activity F, using the same structures. Write the structures on the board if learners need help. On one side of the card they write the message, on the other side they draw a picture of the place the writer is sending it from. Encourage learners to be imaginative.

Look at the pictures. Tell the story.

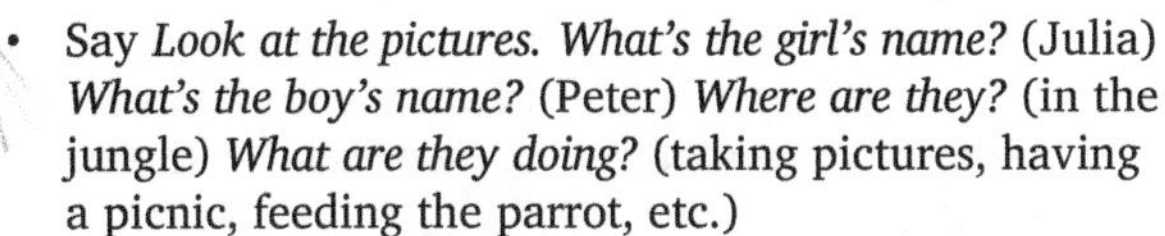

- Say *Look at the pictures. What's the girl's name?* (Julia) *What's the boy's name?* (Peter) *Where are they?* (in the jungle) *What are they doing?* (taking pictures, having a picnic, feeding the parrot, etc.)
- Say *These pictures tell a story. The name of the story is 'The picnic and the parrot'.* Learners look at the pictures. Say *Point to the first picture. This is Julia and Peter. They're going for a walk. Julia is saying,'Look at the beautiful waterfall. Let's have our picnic here.' Now you tell the story.*
- In pairs or small groups, learners take turns to talk about what they can see in the pictures. Check ideas in open class, asking groups to suggest sentences to make as complete a story as possible.
- To give learners more support, you can write the following prompts on the board:

Picture 2: Where are Julia's feet?
What is Peter doing?
Picture 3: What are the children doing now?
What is in the sky?
Picture 4: Where is the parrot now?
What are the children doing?

Suggested answers

Julia's feet are in the water.
Peter's taking a photo.
The children are having a picnic.
There's a parrot in the sky.
The parrot is on Julia's head now.
Peter is giving the parrot some food!
The children are laughing.

Test tip: MOVERS
Speaking (Part 2)

✔ Learners see four pictures. The examiner starts the story by saying its title and talking about what's happening in the first picture. Learners then continue telling the story by talking about what's happening in pictures two, three and four.
Make this easier for learners by training them to imagine they are just answering two or three questions about each picture, e.g. *What's he/she doing now? Who's holding the … now? Where's … now?* Also tell them it is fine to use the present tense.

➜ Take every opportunity to practise this by asking *What, Where, Who, Why* or *How many* questions about any story or activity picture in the book that learners are finding interesting. See the questions for the picture in Activity G for examples of this. You can also ask:
How many children can you see?
How many bags/clouds/rocks/birds can you see?
Where are the children sitting?
Who is taking a photo?
Who has her feet in the water? etc.

Extension

Use the last picture in Activity G as a Reading and Writing Part 6 practice task. Ask *What can you see in the picture? Write three or four sentences.* Learners work in pairs. Walk around and help with vocabulary if necessary.

H Listen and colour the picture on page 13.

- Learners look at the black and white picture on page 13. Ask *Who can you see in this picture?* (Jim, Grace, Mr and Mrs Star) *What are they doing?* (sitting down, talking)
- Play an 'I Spy' game, looking at the picture. Say *I see something beginning with R. What is it?* (a rock) Learners guess until they say the object you are thinking of. Repeat several times with different words.

06

- Check learners have colouring pencils or crayons. Say *Listen. A man is telling a boy to colour some things in this picture. Listen and colour five things in this picture.* Play the audio. Pause between each instruction so learners have enough time to colour the correct objects.

Tapescript:

Boy:	Can I colour some parts of this picture?
Man:	Yes. Find the smaller rock first.
Boy:	OK. Shall I colour it green?
Man:	Yes. Good idea!
Man:	There's a little snail in this picture. Can you see it?
Boy:	Wait ... Oh yes! On the ground. Shall I colour that, too?
Man:	Yes, please. Colour it grey ... No ... pink is nicer. Make it that colour.
Boy:	All right.
Boy:	What now? Can I colour one of the leaves? The one on Jim's hat?
Man:	Not that one. Colour the one in the water.
Boy:	Fine. How about orange for that?
Man:	OK! Great! Thank you.
Man:	Now colour the bottle, please.
Boy:	The one that Grace is holding?
Man:	That's right. Make it blue.
Boy:	OK. That's easy. There!
Boy:	Can I colour Grace's net, too?
Man:	Yes. She likes fishing in this river, I think.
Boy:	I enjoy doing that sometimes. Can I choose the colour?
Man:	Yes.
Boy:	Brilliant! There! It's red now.
Man:	Thank you.

- Ask *What did you colour? What colour is it? Did you colour the bigger or smaller rock? Did you colour the leaf on Jim's hat or the leaf in the water?* Check answers with the class.

Answers

smaller rock – green
snail on ground – pink
leaf in the water – orange
girl's water bottle – blue
fishing net – red

Test tip: MOVERS
Listening (Part 5)

✔ Learners listen and colour four parts of the picture. They do not need to finish colouring each part. Make sure learners understand that they only need to show they have understood which part of the picture they should colour and which colour to use. They don't get any extra marks for beautiful colouring!

➜ Make sure that learners know all the YLE colours they are likely to hear: blue, brown, green, grey, orange, pink, purple, red and yellow. They will not be asked to colour anything white or black.

Use line drawings in the book or other line drawings you have and give simple colouring instructions. Learners could also do this in pairs.

Explain that colouring instructions are not always the same as real-world colours, e.g. *Can you see the dolphin? Colour it green.*

I Listen and sing the song.

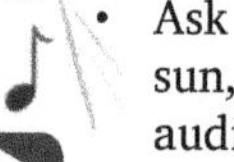
07

- Ask *What can you see in the picture?* (grass, sky, the sun, a boy, bees, a rock, flowers, butterflies) Play the audio. Learners listen to the song and read the words.
- Play the audio again. Learners sing the song. You could add actions to make this more fun and memorable. Learners stand, then sit down again when they sing *sit* in the first verse; they point to the sky when they sing *sky* in the second verse; they draw a circle in the air when they sing *sun* in the third verse.

37

- You can also play a version of this song without the words for learners to sing along to.

2 *Let's have fun!*

Plan a picnic and make a poster.

Say *Look at page 68, Activity 2.* Ask *What is the information about?* (a picnic) *What time is the picnic?* (half past three) *What should you bring?* (food and drink)

Give each learner a copy of Photocopy 2 (TB page 55). Put learners into groups of four or five. Say *Now plan your picnic.* Write a gapped summary on the board for groups to copy and complete:

The picnic is on ____________ in ____________. You can see animals like ____________ there! We can travel there by ____________. We must take ____________ and ____________ to eat. Bring some ____________ too! After our picnic, we can ____________.

Help groups with vocabulary if necessary. After groups have made their decisions and written a plan, they draw their picnic. Choose at least two groups to tell the class about their plan.

Let's speak!

What can you see in the countryside? Listen to your friend and draw.

Learners look at Activity 2 on page 72. Read the speech bubble together. As a class, brainstorm things you can see in the countryside. Draw a mind map on the board with 'The countryside' at the centre and four branches labelled: Animals, Plants, People, Things. You could ask learners to write their ideas on the board, checking their spelling, or do this yourself.

Demonstrate the speaking activity with one learner in open class, saying *I can see a …* Learners then take turns to ask and answer questions about the countryside in closed pairs. Ask different pairs to tell the class what they said/drew.

Ask learners to report back in open class.

29

 ***Let's say!***

Say *Look at page 74, Activity 2. Listen.*
Play the audio. Learners listen.
Say *Let's say /s/. Sue, Grace, cycle, circle, sun.* Learners repeat. Say *Tell me more English words with /s/.* Learners answer (e.g. *supermarket, silly, circus, salad*). Learners listen again to the audio, repeating the rhyme as fast as they can.

Home FUN booklet

Pages 22–23 and 28–29 school, the world around us

Picture dictionary: world around us

Go online

to practise your English
to listen to the audio recordings
to find more FUN activities!

3 Daisy's tiger dream

Main topics:	home, animals, the natural world
Story summary:	Daisy has cool clothes and lots of possessions, but she isn't happy. One night she has a dream which changes everything.
Main grammar:	comparative adjectives, *can, could/couldn't, be good at*
Main vocabulary:	*across, balcony, brave, brilliant, busy, cave, comic, computer game, count* (v), *dream* (n), *exciting, frightened, guitar, hear, kind* (adj), *kitten, light, moon, mouth, movie, near, quietly, roller skates, sail* (v), *smile, star, steps, strange, tiger, wind*
Value:	Being a good friend (*"I can be a good friend."*)
***Let's say!*:**	/aɪ/
Practice tasks:	Reading and Writing Part 3 (A), Reading and Writing Part 6 (E), Listening Part 5 (G)
Test tasks:	Speaking Part 3 (G), Listening Part 2 (H)

Equipment:

- audio: Story, C, G, H
- presentation PLUS flashcards
  Go to Presentation plus to find pictures of Movers vocabulary from Unit 3. You can use the pictures to teach/review important words in this unit.
- presentation PLUS Image carousel 14–17 (roller skates, skateboard, steps, cave): Storytelling
- Photocopy 3 (TB page 56) (one per pair, cut into cards): D Extension
- crayons / colouring pencils: G

Storytelling

Before listening

With books closed …

- Introduce the topic of the story. Write *bedroom* on the board. Ask *What can you do here?* (play with toys, sleep, read) Say *This story is about a girl. She has lots of things. Are children with lots of things always happy?* Ask *When are you happy?* Write some of their answers on the board. For example *when I'm with friends / when I go on holiday.*
- Review/Teach *roller skates, cave, skateboard* and *steps.* Show these pictures from the Image carousel. Say *Steps are outside a building. Stairs are inside a building.* Check understanding with simple questions. Ask *Are there any steps outside your school? Which animals live in a cave?* (bats, bears) Teach *light* by pointing to one in the classroom. Say *We can talk about the light from the sun or the light from the moon, too.* Write all the new words on the board and leave them there for reference.
- Learners look at the story pictures (with or without the text) from the Image carousel or on page 20. Ask *What's the girl's name?* (Daisy) *In the first picture, is the girl awake?* (yes) *What's she thinking about?* (a skateboard, a bike, computer games) *In the second picture, is she awake?* (No, she's sleeping.) Check they understand *dream.* Ask *Do you dream when you are awake or asleep?* (asleep) *What do you dream about?* Learners suggest ideas. *What's she dreaming about?* Learners guess.
- Say *Now let's listen to the story. Look at page 20.*

Listening

With books open …

08

Play the audio or read the story. Learners listen.

Play the audio or read the story again.

- Pause after *She counted the steps: 44, 45 … 61, 62 … 97, 98, 99, 100!* on page 21. Ask *Was Daisy a happy child?* (no) *What did Daisy see in her dream?* (a lake, a mountain, the moon, stars, a cave) *What did she see in the cave?* (some steps) *Did she go down the steps?* (yes)
- Pause again after *Her friends never called her before breakfast!* on page 22. Ask *What kind of animal did Daisy see in the cave?* (a tiger) *Did the tiger help Daisy?* (yes) *What did Daisy hear when she woke up?* (her phone)

After listening

- Ask *Who wanted Daisy to help him?* (Jack) *What was Daisy's new pet?* (a kitten) *What colour was it?* (black and orange)
- Ask *Why was Daisy happy at the end of the story?* (She could help a friend. She could be kind to an animal. It was a sunny day.)

Value

- Ask learners to think about the dream. Ask *What's more important: toys or friends? Being cool or being kind? Helping other people or having new laptops and phones?* Continue the discussion in L1 if necessary. Ask *How can we be kind to our classmates?* (We can teach classmates to do things we're good at, we can help them with homework.)

Read and write the correct word.

- Say *That night, Daisy had a strange ...* (dream) Learners look at the example. Tell them to cover the coloured words and read all the sentences and guess the answers in pairs. Then they look at the words and complete the activity. Check answers in open class, correcting pronunciation when necessary.

Answers

2 stars **3** sailed **4** busy **5** outside **6** pretty

Draw lines and make sentences.

- Learners read the instruction and look at the example. Ask *What did Daisy want to be?* (happier)
- Working individually, learners draw lines to match the two halves of the sentences. Fast finishers can compare answers. If they have any that are different they can check again in the story while the rest of the class finish.
- Ask *Which sentence comes first in the story?* (Daisy wanted to be happier.) Tell learners to number the sentences 1–6 so they show the events in the correct order. (1, 2, 6, 3, 4, 5) Ask volunteers to retell the story in order, using the sentences.

Answers

2 saw a sailing boat. **3** Daisy very slowly. **4** Jack phoned her. **5** Daisy a kitten. **6** bottom of the steps.

Extension

Learners each write a sentence about the story with a word missing and two options to complete it, e.g. *Daisy's mother gave Daisy a) a kitten b) a tiger*. Learners swap with a partner, who decides which is correct. Ask volunteers to write their sentences on the board for the class to guess.

Who's talking about this story? Listen and tick (✓) the box.

- Remind learners of the value discussion when they first read the story (see above) or discuss the value now for the first time.

09

- Learners look at the pictures of the three children. Ask *Are these children boys or girls?* (two boys, one girl) Play the audio. Ask *What are their names?* (Alice, Ben and Jim) Check pronunciation.
- Say *Each child is talking about a different story. Which child read 'Daisy's tiger dream'?* Play the audio again. Learners listen and decide. Ask *Was it Alice? Was it Ben? Was it Jim?* Learners put up their hands to show which answer they think is right. Check answers.
- Play the audio so learners can listen to Alice again.

Ask *What has Daisy got at the end of Alice's story?* (more toys and a new phone) *What has she got at the end of our story?* (a kitten) Play Jim's part of the recording again. Ask *What can Daisy play at the end of Jim's story?* (her new guitar) *Who has a new guitar in our story?* (Jack)

Answer

Ben

Tapescript:

Alice:	Hi! My name's Alice. I'm nine and I liked this story a lot because Daisy's happy. She's got more toys and a new phone at the end of the story.
Ben:	Hello! My name's Ben. I'm ten. In this story, the girl ... her name's Daisy ... understands she doesn't need a better bike. She's happy because she's got a new friend.
Jim:	I'm Jim. I like reading stories like this one. It was brilliant! Daisy can play her new guitar and learns to do lots of exciting things. She's really cool.

Complete the sentences with *-er* or *more*.

- Draw two books of different sizes on the board. Ask *Which book is smaller?* Learners point to the smaller book. Say *This book is smaller than that book.* Point to the bigger book and say *This book is bigger than that book.*
- Write the sentences with comparative adjectives under the drawings. Show learners we add *-er* to *small* and *big*.
- Point to other objects in the classroom and ask similar questions with *nice, old, short, long,* etc.
- Don't focus on the written forms, as some of these will be irregular. Just practise adding the *-er* ending in spoken forms.
- Draw two flowers on the board: a beautiful one and a drooping one with only a few petals. Say *This flower is more beautiful than that flower.* Write the sentence on the board. Show learners that with longer words, we use *more*, not *-er*.
- Learners look at the pictures in Activity D. Ask *Which TV is newer? Which is older? Which guitar is louder? Which guitar is quieter? Which cat is younger? Which cat is older?* Learners point to the correct pictures. Look together at the two examples. In pairs, learners complete sentences 3–7, using the drawings and adjectives in brackets to help them.
- Check answers in open class.

Answers

3 newer **4** more boring **5** louder **6** more difficult **7** younger

Extension

- Say *Work in pairs*. Give a set of cards of 'Funny sentences!' (Photocopy 3, TB page 56) to each pair. Pairs should have 14 object cards and 10 comparative adjective cards.
- Say *Play the game. Make funny sentences!* Pairs work together to divide the cards into seven sets of three cards (object card + comparative card + object card) to make the structure of a sentence. They lay these in rows on their desk or table. There are three extra comparative adjectives to give more possibilities.
- Suggested sentences: *A kangaroo is taller than a kitten. A whale is more beautiful than a shark. A kite is longer than a scarf. A man is older than a boy. A piano is quieter than a guitar. A girl is younger than a woman. A computer game is more exciting than a CD.* With this combination, *funnier, stronger* and *more boring* are not used.

E Complete the sentences.

- Ask *In the story, when Daisy was in bed, she wasn't happy. What did she want?* Learners find the sentence on Student's Book page 20. (a longer skateboard, a better bike, more exciting games, a newer laptop) Write on the board *I can ask Mum and Dad to buy me a longer skateboard.*
- Learners look at the two examples about Daisy and Jack. Ask *Did Daisy get a new guitar?* (yes) *Did Jack get a new jacket?* (no)
- Say *When I was a child, I asked my dad to buy me a bike. He said yes!* Look happy. Say *And I asked my mum to buy me a horse. She said no!* Look unhappy. Write on the board *I asked my dad to buy me a bike. I asked my mum to buy me a horse.*
- Ask *Last week, did you ask your parents to buy you things? What did you ask for?* Learners answer, using the model structure on the board. Put a list of some of the objects learners wanted on the board.
- In pairs, learners talk about three things that they wanted using the same structure.
- Learners complete sentences 3–5 in the activity and write the result (*He/She said yes/no!*). They can draw happy or sad faces.
- Different learners then read one of their sentences in open class, e.g. *I asked my brother to buy me an ice cream. He said no!* Check the pronunciation of *said*. Explain that it rhymes with *bed*.

Test tip: MOVERS
Reading and Writing (all parts)

✔ Encourage learners to answer all of the tasks, even if their answers are guesses.

F Read the text. Choose the right words and write them on the lines.

- Learners look at the picture of Daisy and Jack. Ask *Is Daisy happy?* (yes) *What's she doing?* (playing the guitar, helping Jack)
- Learners read the text without adding the missing words. Ask *Where did Daisy go in the afternoon?* (to Jack's house)
- Tell learners to read the instruction. Ask *How many words are there for each answer?* (three) Say *Two of these words are wrong. Only one word is right.* In pairs or on their own, learners choose and write the correct answers.
- Check answers in open class.

Answers

2 to **3** our **4** newer **5** at **6** of **7** need

G Which one is different? Look and say.

- Draw simple pictures of a lamp, a phone, rain and a chair on the board. Say *Now tell me about these four pictures. Which one is different?* Prompt a reply. Say *The rain is different. Why? You find a lamp, a phone and a chair inside a house. You don't find rain inside a house!*
- Learners look at the first set of pictures. Ask *What can you see?* (a tomato, a skateboard, a boat, a pencil) Ask a learner to read out the speech bubble. Ask *Which picture is different?* (the boat)
- Check understanding. Ask *Why is the boat different?* (It's green.) Write on the board *The tomato, the skateboard and the pencil are red. The boat is different. It's green.*
- In pairs, learners look at sets 2–4 and find ways to explain the differences. Help by prompting as needed. Check answers with the class, accepting all valid answers.

Suggested answers

2 The boy, the woman and the man are happy. The girl is different. She's sad.
3 You wear roller skates, a sweater and shoes. The milk is different. You drink milk.
4 The kitten, the tiger and the lion have legs. The whale is different. It doesn't have legs.

Test tip: MOVERS
Speaking (Part 3)

✔ Learners have to say why one picture is different from three others.
➜ Teach learners a simple way to explain a difference in noun sets, e.g *The W is different. X, Y and Z are … but W is a … .*

Look at the animals. Listen and colour.

- Check that learners have colouring pencils with all the YLE colours. Say *Now listen to a woman and a boy. The woman is telling the boy to colour three of the animals in Activity G.*
- Play the audio. Learners listen and colour. Play the audio again. Learners finish their colouring. Check answers in open class, asking *Which animal is not coloured in?* (the tiger) *Which animal is purple?* (the whale) *Which animal is pink?* (the kitten) *Which animal is green?* (the lion)

10

Answers

whale – purple
kitten – pink
lion – green
no colour for the tiger

Tapescript:

Woman: Can you colour these four animals?

Boy: Yes, I can.

Woman: Great. Colour the whale first. Colour it purple.

Boy: OK. Can I colour that cool kitten now?

Woman: Yes, you can. Colour it pink, please.

Boy: All right. I'm colouring that picture now.

Woman: Great!

Woman: Now colour the ...

Boy: Tiger?

Woman: No. The lion, please.

Boy: OK. Shall I make it green?

Woman: That's a funny colour for that kind of animal, but OK!

Boy: Thanks!

Extension

Learners draw two 'Which one is different?' sets of their own. They draw and colour a picture for each thing and write sentences about the set as in the suggested answers on page 26. Display some of these around the classroom.

Test tip: MOVERS
Listening (Part 5)

✔ Learners might see two objects that are the same in the picture. These might be of different sizes or be in different places. Learners need to listen carefully so they hear which one to colour.

➜ Use line drawings of paired objects and give colouring instructions. Say, e.g. *Colour the book. Make it orange. Don't colour the bigger book. Colour the smaller book. Colour the pencil now. Don't colour the pencil that's on the desk. Colour the pencil that's on the floor. Make that pencil green.*

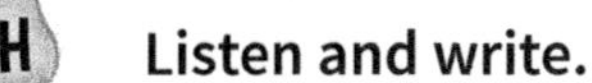

Listen and write.

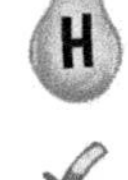

- Ask *What is Daisy holding?* (her kitten) Say *Listen to Daisy. She's talking to Mr Pool about her new pet. Look at the form.* Ask *What's the kitten's name?* (Tiger) Ask questions to encourage learners to predict the rest of the answers, e.g. *What do you think Tiger enjoys playing with?* Accept any valid suggestions.

- Play the audio twice. Learners listen and write the answers. Check answers in open class.

Answers

1 scarf **2** climbing **3** fish **4** seat **5** food

Tapescript:

Man: Hi, Daisy! You've got a new kitten!

Daisy: Yes, Mr Pool. I love it!

Man: What's its name?

Daisy: Tiger!

Man: Tiger? What a brilliant name!

Can you see the answer? Now you listen and write.

1 Daisy: I play with it a lot! We have lots of fun.

Man: Good! Kittens like that. What does it like playing with?

Daisy: My old scarf. Tiger carries it around the house in its mouth.

Man: An old scarf? That's funny.

2 Daisy: Tiger's really good at something ...

Man: Um, what?

Daisy: Climbing! Yes, it can climb up the back of Dad's armchair!

Man: Wow!

3 Man: What does Tiger like eating?

Daisy: Lots of fish. It doesn't like meat.

Man: Oh, I'm surprised. But fish is very good for all kinds of cats.

Daisy: Yes, I know ... Mum told me that.

4 Man: Does your kitten sleep a lot in the day?

Daisy: Yes!

Man: Where does it sleep? In a box?

Daisy: No. On a seat. I like sitting on that seat, too. It's outside in our garden.

Man: Nice!

5 Man: And is your kitten clever? Can it understand you?

Daisy: It understands one word. It comes when I call 'Food! Food!'.

Man: Well, that's good!

Daisy: Can cats learn lots of words, Mr Pool?

Man: Well, it's easier to teach dogs, but you can try!

Daisy: OK! Bye!

Let's talk about friends. Ask and answer questions with a friend.

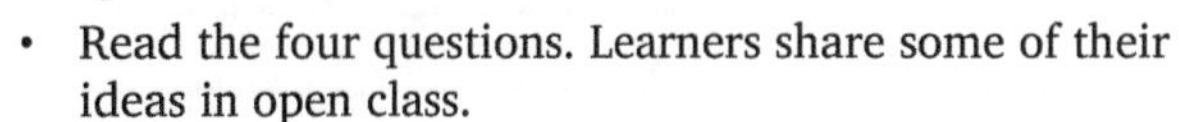

- Read the four questions. Learners share some of their ideas in open class.
- Say *Work in pairs.* Learners ask and answer the questions.
- Some pairs share their answers in open class.

Let's have fun!

Draw and talk about mountains.

Say *Look at page 69, Activity 3.* Ask *What can you see?* (mountains, sky) Learners copy the picture in their notebooks. Explain in L1 that they should imagine they are in their mountain picture. Ask *What can you see above you? Below you? Can you see any caves? What's in the cave? What's the weather like? Can you see any forests? Rivers? Lakes?*

Learners add their ideas to their mountain picture. Give them time to colour it if possible. When they have finished drawing, learners could either describe it to a partner or answer their classmates' questions about it in open class.

Let's speak!

Play the game. Make and say funny sentences.

Say *Look at page 72, Activity 3.* Read the speech bubbles together. Write on the board:

... is ...er than ...

... is more ... than ...

Say *Now you make funny sentences.* As a class, learners suggest ideas. Praise creative and funny suggestions, e.g. *A penguin is cleverer than a pencil!* In pairs, learners continue to make funny comparisons, writing down their favourite one. At the end, ask each pair to report one sentence to the class. The class votes on which sentence is funniest.

30

Let's say!

Say *Look at page 74, Activity 3. Listen.*
Play the audio. Learners listen.
Say *Let's say* /aɪ/. *Kind, tiger, bike, night, light.* Learners repeat. Say *Tell me more English words with this sound.* Learners answer (e.g. *my, sky, eye, bye*). Learners listen again to the audio, repeating the rhyme as fast as they can.

Home FUN booklet

Pages 2–3 and 14–15 animals, the home

Picture dictionary: animals

Go online

to practise your English
to listen to the audio recordings
to find more FUN activities!

4 A busy Monday

Main topics:	home, activities at home
Story summary:	It's too snowy to go out. Mark, his family and his friend Alex do some things to stay busy.
Main grammar:	*must*, simple past regular and irregular, *How about …?*
Main vocabulary:	*asleep, awake, basement, cage, call* (v), *cinema, circus, clean* (v), *cook* (n), *dangerous, dentist, e-book, email* (v), *everything, fall, fantastic, feed* (v), *fun, funfair, hall, hooray, kangaroo, library, lion, meat, model* (adj), *paint* (v), *panda, parrot, piano, plant* (n), *practice, practise, puppy, rug, safe, scarf, snow, soup, spaceship, sports centre, supermarket, sweater, text* (n), *tidy* (v), *video* (v), *washing machine, water* (v), *zebra*
Value:	Being productive (*"I like being busy!"*)
***Let's say!*:**	/d/, /t/
Practice tasks:	Reading and Writing Part 1 (A), Reading and Writing Part 6 (H)
Test tasks:	Reading and Writing Part 3 (E), Listening Part 4 (G)

Equipment:

- audio: Story, F, G, I
- presentation PLUS flashcards
  Go to Presentation plus to find pictures of Movers vocabulary from Unit 4. You can use the pictures to teach/review important words in this unit.
- presentation PLUS Image carousel 18–20 (house, parrot, kitchen): Storytelling
- Photocopy 4 (TB page 57) (one per learner): Let's have fun!
- crayons / colouring pencils: C, Let's have fun!

Storytelling

Before listening

With books closed …

- Introduce the topic of the story. Show learners the photographs of the house, kitchen and parrot from the Image carousel. Ask *What is this?* (a house) *Do you live in a house or a flat? What do you do at home when it's raining or snowing? Do you enjoy playing computer games / making models? What can you do in a kitchen?* (eat, cook) *What bird is this?* (a parrot) Say *This story is about a family who can't go outside because it's snowing.*
- Review/Teach the days of the week and places in town: *sports centre, circus, café, supermarket, cinema*. Check understanding of *busy* by miming someone doing more than one activity at the same time, e.g. cooking, talking on the phone and cleaning.
- Look at the first story picture (with or without the text) from the Image carousel or on page 28. Ask *Are there buildings like this in our town?* Learners answer. *Which day is it?* Learners guess, e.g. Monday. *What's the weather like?* (It's snowing.)
- Say *Now let's listen to the story. Look at page 28.*

Listening

With books open …

12

- Play the audio or read the story. Learners listen.
- Play the audio or read the story again.
- Pause after *I read his message and sent him a quick answer.* on page 29. Ask *Why can't Mark go to school?* (It's snowing.) *Why can't his mum and dad go to work?* (The roads are dangerous.) *What's Mark's mum's job?* (a dentist) *What's Mark's dad's job?* (a cook) Ask *What would Mark's mum like to do today?* (make a meat and potato pie, paint the hall, clean the hall rug, water all the plants) Ask *What would Mark's dad like to do?* (fix the washing machine, then make some bread and some onion soup and then read his new e-book) *What must Mark do?* (clean the pet rabbit's cage, feed the puppy and practise the piano. He can also make a model spaceship.) *Who is Alex?* (Mark's best friend)
- Pause again after *Dad cleaned his football boots and tidied the basement.* on page 31. Ask *Why didn't they feed the puppy?* (It was asleep.) *Why couldn't they make the model spaceship?* (They couldn't find four small pieces.) *Which animals are in the computer game?* (kangaroo, lion, zebra and panda)
- At the end of the story, ask *What did they teach the parrot?* (to say 'Busy Day!') *What did Mark's dad find in the washing machine?* (the four missing pieces of the model spaceship)

After listening

- Ask *Did Mark have a quiet day or a busy day?* (a busy day) *How many things did he do?* Learners list all the activities they remember from the story.

 **Value**

- Say *Look at page 31.* Point to Dad and Mum and say *Mark's family had a busy day.* Ask *Do you like busy days? What do you prefer: busy days or quiet days? How do you feel when you're busy?* Learners answer in English or L1.

A Read and write the correct number.

- Learners look at the coloured words, then find and circle them in the story. Look at the example. In pairs, learners match the words to the definitions by writing the correct number. Check answers in open class.

Answers

2 asleep **3** machine **4** to video **5** cook **6** awake

Extension

In small groups, learners mime the words from Activity A for their classmates to guess. When they have done the words from Activity A, they can use other words from the story, too.

B Read and answer the questions.

- Write on the board __________? *Alex.* Say *The answer is Alex. What's the question?* Accept any possible answers, e.g. *Who is Mark's best friend? Who did Mark text? Who helped Mark clean the rabbit's cage?*
- Write on the board __________? *Monday.* Say *The answer is Monday. What's the question?* Accept any possible answers, e.g. *What day is it today?*
- Learners look at the example in Activity B. Say *Look at more questions about the story. Can you complete the answers?* In pairs, learners write the answers. Check in open class.
- Ask further questions, e.g. *What colour did Mark's mum paint the hall?* Learners guess. *Do you like onion soup? Have you got a basement in your house or flat? Have you got a hall?*

Answers

2 spaceship **3** hall **4** onion **5** basement **6** scarf

C Read and colour the best answer green.

- Remind learners of the value discussion when they first read the story (see above) or discuss the value now for the first time.
- Read Mark's speech bubble with learners. Ask *Which answer is best, A, B or C? Colour it green.* In pairs, learners choose the right answer and colour it (make sure they have a green colouring pencil ot crayon).
- Check answers by asking a pair to read the complete conversation.
- Ask *What other answers can you say?* (That's great! Fantastic! Me too!) Learners role play the conversation again, using their own answers.
- Review/Teach *to tidy* by miming tidying a desk. Ask *What jobs do you do at home? Do you help to cook / wash plates / tidy / clean the house?* List the jobs they do on the board, e.g. *wash my bike, read a story to my baby brother, tidy my room.* Leave learners' suggestions on the board (for use in Activity D). Ask *How do you feel when you have lots of things to do? How do you feel when you finish them?*

Answer

C

Extension

Write the structures below on the board. Learners copy them in their notebooks and complete them for homework. Ask them to illustrate each sentence with a picture. If necessary, preteach *tomorrow*.

Today was good. I ______, ______ and ______ .
Tomorrow, I can ______ and ______ and ______ .

D What must you do this week? Write five things.

- Review/Teach *must* by saying three sentences about yourself, e.g. *This week I must go to the supermarket, I must clean my car and I must find my glasses!* Ask *What must I do? I must …* Learners list your jobs. *What must Mark do in the story? He must …* (clean his rabbit's cage, feed the puppy, practise the piano)
- Ask *What things must you do this week?* Learners suggest ideas for themselves, using the suggestions on the board from Activity C if needed. Give some more examples, e.g. *I must fix my bike, I must tidy my room, I must find a missing jigsaw piece, I must do my homework,* etc.
- Learners write sentences with five activities to complete Activity D. In small groups, they compare their answers. Check in open class.

E Read the story. Choose a word from the box. Write the correct word next to numbers 1–5.

- Say *Let's read another story about Mark.* Read the example sentence together. Ask *What does Mark want to be?* (a cook) *What does Mark want to make?* (lunch) Say *Can you see the words?* Learners point to the words under the pictures. Say *These are the answers. Write the answers in the spaces. You only need five of them.* Make sure learners understand that there are extra words.
- Check the answers for 1 to 5 in open class.

Now choose the best name for the story. Tick (✔) one box.

- Read the story titles in 6 aloud. In pairs, learners decide on the best title and tick the box. Ask learners to vote for their choice.

Answers

1 vegetables **2** floor **3** scored **4** message **5** hot
6 Mark makes lunch

Test tip: MOVERS
Reading and Writing (Part 3)

✔ Learners choose the correct title for a story from a choice of three.
Before learners complete the text with the five missing words and choose the title, encourage them to read the whole text to get a general understanding of the story.
➔ Ask learners to choose from one right and one wrong title you have written for other short texts, poems or songs. Ask why one is right and the other is wrong. You might also ask learners to think of good alternative titles for all the stories in the book! Ask questions like *Who's the most important person in this story?* to help learners develop this skill.

Extension

Talk about cooking with the class. Write the following questions on the board for learners to discuss in small groups. Feed back in open class.
Do you make lunch for your family?
What can you cook?
Are you good at cooking?
Is learning to cook important?
Who is the best cook in your house?

F Listen and draw lines.

- Review/Teach the six animals in the pictures. Point to the pictures and ask *What's this?* (a horse, a kangaroo, a rabbit, a zebra, a lion, a penguin) *How do you spell it?* (H-O-R-S-E, etc.)
- Say *Listen to the instructions for the game! Draw lines to match the animals to the places.* Play the audio twice. (13)
- Check answers by asking different learners to say where one of the animals is, e.g. *The kangaroo is in the cinema.*

Answers

Lines between:
1 the kangaroo and the cinema
2 the horse and the car park
3 the rabbit and the market
4 the zebra and the pool
5 the lion and the library
6 the penguin and the café

Tapescript:

Move the kangaroo to the cinema.
Move the horse to the car park.
Move the rabbit to the market.
Move the zebra to the pool.
Move the lion to the library.
Move the penguin to the café.

G Listen and tick (✔) the box.

- Learners look at the 18 pictures. Write the following on the board to put in a question: *bat, lift, soup, panda, funfair, noodles.* Ask *In which picture can you see ...?* Learners point to the picture.
- Play the example on the audio, then pause. Ask *What does Jack want for lunch?* (Jack wants soup for lunch.) Learners read the five questions. Say *Now listen and tick the right answer to the other questions.* Play the rest of the audio twice. (14)
- Check answers in open class.

Answers

1 C **2** A **3** B **4** C **5** B

Tapescript:

Example

What does Jack want for lunch?

Mum: Would you like some noodles for lunch today, Jack?

Boy: No, thanks, Mum. Can I have some of the vegetable soup that you made?

Mum: All right. And some cheese?

Boy: No, but I'd like some of that nice bread, please.

Mum: OK.

Can you see the tick? Now you listen and tick the box.

1 Who's Julia sending a text to?

Boy: Who are you texting, Julia?

Girl: My new friend. She's coming to play with us now.

Boy: The one with the fair hair and glasses?

Girl: She doesn't need those now and she's got curly brown hair.

Boy: Oh, I know. She's fun! Good!

2 What's Mum doing now?

Boy: What's Mum doing now? Is she making lunch?

Dad: No, I think she's planting something outside.

Boy: I looked there.

Dad: Oh, I know. She's upstairs looking at her new e-book.

Boy: Right.

3 What's in Charlie's video?

Girl: I've got a really cool video on my phone, Mum. Come and see!

Mum: What's in it, Charlie? Not another kitten?

Girl: No, it's a panda. Look!

Mum: Oh ... It's really sweet.

Girl: Yes ... not scary like the one of the bat we saw on TV.

4 Where's Grandpa this afternoon?

Boy: I'd like to go to the cinema on Tuesday.

Girl: Me too. Grandpa saw a good film there last Sunday.

Boy: Did he? Where is he now? He's often at the library on Fridays.

Girl: Yes! But he called Mum after lunch. He's at the funfair!
Boy: Wow!

5 What's Dad fixing now?
Boy: What's Dad fixing now? The lift?
Girl: No, that's OK now. The shower, I think.
Boy: Oh, great. I want him to help me fix the school website, too.
Girl: Go and tell him, then.

Test tip: MOVERS
Listening (Part 4)

✔ When learners are listening for the correct answer, words or phrases like *No, Not today, Sorry, We can't ...* might signal that an option heard in the previous turn is wrong. Words or phrases like *Yes, All right, Good idea! OK* might signal that an option just heard is the right answer!

➜ Train learners to listen carefully for these positive or negative words or phrases in conversations. Pause the audio when you hear examples of them and write them on the board. Check understanding by asking, e.g. *So can the boy eat that? Why? / Why not?*

Look at the picture. Complete the sentences and answer the questions.

- Learners look at the picture. Ask *Where are these people?* (in a café) *How many people can you see?* (three) *What is the boy eating?* (a sandwich) *What is the girl holding?* (a drink) *What colour is the man's sweater?* (green) *Is the table round or square?* (round) *What's the weather like?* (windy)
- Ask *What's on the wall behind the man's head?* (a mirror) Look at the examples. Read the them together. Make sure learners understand that there might be more than one way to complete the sentences and answer the two questions, and that they can write short or long answers. In pairs, learners complete the sentences and answer the questions. They compare their answers in small groups, before checking in open class.

Suggested answers

1 a (black) bike
2 (green) sweater and (black) trousers
3 a girl and a boy / two children
4 cakes, drinks, sandwiches, fruit

Test tip: MOVERS
Reading and Writing (Part 6)

✔ Learners complete sentences and answer questions about a picture. They can write more than one word if they want. There is often more than one way to complete the sentences or answer the questions.

➜ Use any picture in the book to encourage learners to think of different ways to complete a sentence about the picture, e.g. *The man is wearing ..., That house has ...*

15

Listen and say the poem.

- Point to the picture and say *Look at the girl.* Ask *Where is she?* (in a car) *What's she holding?* (a phone)
- Play the audio, then read the poem together, with learners taking turns to read out lines. Show learners actions for words in the poem. Say and mime *swimming pool* (move your arms to show swimming), *go slow* (pat the air as if to suggest 'slower' and look worried), *looks up, round and down* (look up, round and down), *my friends* (look left and right and smile), *no fun at all* (look angry).
- Learners work in small groups and practise their version of the action poem. Ask groups to perform for the class.

Tapescript:
See Student's Book page 35

Extension

Say *Imagine your mum or dad is driving you through the town. What can you see?* In pairs, learners mime phoning each other, talking about what each of them can see.

Let's have fun!

Design a computer game. What must players do? Tell your classmates.

Learners look at page 69, Activity 4. Ask *Do you play computer games? What can you see in the computer game?* Review/Teach *player, click, press enter, quit, arrow keys.*

Give each learner a copy of Photocopy 4 (TB page 57). Point to the computer game illustration. Ask *What must the players do?* Learners guess. Read the text together. Ask again *What must the players do?* (find the stars) *Where can they go?* (up and down) *Can you move them?* (yes)

In pairs, learners plan and write about a new computer game, using the *You must ...* structure. They then draw a picture. Circulate and help as necessary.

Choose a few learners to share their ideas with the class.

Let's speak!

What can we do? Talk to your friend.

Learners look at page 72, Activity 4. Read the speech bubbles together. Ask *Where are the children?* Learners guess. Ask *What's the matter?* (It's boring.) Write on the board *How about ...ing ...?* Ask learners to make suggestions for really fun things to do. Check they are using the correct *-ing* form (*How about going .../playing .../making ...?* etc.). Encourage learners to use their imaginations and praise creative ideas (*How about making spaceships? How about climbing a tree? How about cooking a monster cake?*). Make a list on the board and vote at the end for the best idea. In pairs, learners role play the conversation and plan a busy day of activities.

31

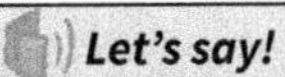

Let's say!

Say *Look at page 74, Activity 4. Listen.*
Play the audio. Learners listen.
Say *Let's say* /t/ *tomato, helped.* Learners repeat. Say *Tell me more English words with* /t/. Learners answer (e.g. *tiger, teacher, table, teddy, laughed*). Say *Now let's say* /d/ *Dad, donkey, carried.* Learners repeat. Say *Tell me more English words with* /d/. Learners answer (e.g. *door, desk, doll, dirty*).
Write *-ed* on the board, and under it write *played* on one side and *helped* on the other. Say *Sometimes we pronounce this* /d/ *and sometimes* /t/. *Listen and say* /d/ *or* /t/. Say a list of past simple verbs for learners to identify the sound, e.g. *clapped* /t/, *carried* /d/, *laughed* /t/, *moved* /d/, *worked* /t/.
Learners listen again to the audio, repeating the rhyme as fast as they can.

Home FUN booklet

Pages 8–9 and 20–21 family, time

Picture dictionary: home

Go online

to practise your English
to listen to the audio recordings
to find more FUN activities!

5 The tomango tree

Main topics:	the natural world
Story summary:	Tom's father can't grow fruit on his farm. One day, Tom goes for a walk in the forest and finds the perfect fruit to grow.
Main grammar:	past simple, relative pronoun *where, could/couldn't, too* + adjective
Main vocabulary:	*bat, building, carefully, chicken, city, climb, country, countryside, cow, exciting, farm, fish* (v), *fruit, goat, grow* (v), *hill, hundreds (of), jungle, kind* (n), *lucky, mirror, only, parents, plant* (v), *sea, sheep, show* (v), *suddenly, tall, tractor, vegetable, waterfall, wonderful, work* (v)
Value:	Having a dream for the future (*"One day, I want to …"*)
***Let's say!*:**	/əʊ/
Practice tasks:	Reading and Writing Part 5 (G)
Test tasks:	Listening Part 5 (F), Listening Part 1 (H), Speaking Part 4 (J)

Equipment:

- audio: Story, F, H
- presentation PLUS flashcards
  Go to Presentation plus to find pictures of Movers vocabulary from Unit 5. You can use the pictures to teach/review important words in this unit.
- presentation PLUS Image carousel 21–29
  (fruit farm, forest, waterfall, field, tractor, building, bus stop, shopping centre, street): Storytelling, A
- crayons / colouring pencils: F, Let's have fun!
- real fruit or plastic toy fruit: Storytelling

Storytelling

Before listening

With books closed …

- Introduce the topic of the story. Show learners the photograph of the fruit farm from the Image carousel. Say *Look! What is it?* (a (fruit) farm) Ask learners about fruit. Show them some real or plastic fruit. Ask *What is this? Can you sometimes find this on trees? What's your favourite kind of fruit?* Write learners' favourite fruits on the board. Help with non-YLE vocabulary, e.g. *figs, peaches*, or Flyers-level vocabulary like *strawberries*. Say *This story is about a boy who finds some fruit on a tree.*
- Review/Teach *hear* and *grow*. Use mime to teach *hear*, by cupping your ear. To teach *grow*, draw a picture of a small plant and a bigger plant on the board. Say *This plant is growing.*
- Ask *Where does fruit grow?* (on farms, in forests) *What other things can you see on farms?* (fields, farm buildings, tractors, animals, e.g.cows, sheep, goats, pigs, chickens, etc.)
- Learners look at the first story picture (with or without the text) on the Image carousel or on page 36. Ask *Where's this boy?* (in the countryside / on a farm) *Which animals can you see?* (cow, sheep, goat, chicken) *What's the boy's name?* (Tom) *How old is he?* Learners guess.
- Look at the second story picture. Ask *Where is Tom now?* (in his bedroom) *What can he see from his window?* (a hill, fields, a cow, a tree, a cloud)
- Say *Now let's listen to the story. Look at page 36.*

Listening

With books open …

16

Play the audio or read the story. Learners listen.

Play the audio or read the story again.

- Pause after *'I want to climb it! Yes! Now!'* on page 37. Ask *What did Tom love doing in the countryside?* (going for walks, climbing trees, listening to the birds, fishing) *What did Tom's parents grow?* (vegetables) *What did Tom's father want to grow?* (fruit) *Where's Tom now?* (in the forest / at the top of the hill)
- Pause again after *Then he picked five more and put them in his bag.* on page 38. Ask *What did Tom hear?* (a fruit bat) *What did the strange fruit look like?* (a tomato or mango) *How many did Tom pick altogether?* (eight)

After listening

- After listening to the whole story, ask *What do Tom's parents grow on the farm now?* (tomangoes) *Did Tom find any more tomangoes in the forest?* (no) *Did he see the fruit bat again?* (no) *Was there really a fruit bat in the tree?* Learners guess.

 **Value**

- Ask *What did Tom want to do in the story?* Write a list together on the board, e.g. *Tom wanted to climb the tree. He wanted to climb the hills. He wanted to work on the farm and grow fruit. He wanted to sail down the river and across the sea. He wanted to go to countries where there are mountains, waterfalls and jungles.* Say *Yes, that was Tom's dream.* Ask in L1 *What's your dream? What do you want to do one day?* Learners suggest ideas.

A Write the words (2–9) in the correct box.

- With books closed, draw two big circles on the board. In the centre of one write *city*; in the centre of the other write *countryside*. Ask *What can you see in the city? What can you see in the countryside?* Ask *What words can you remember from the story?* Write learners' suggestions in the circles. Accept any possible answers.
- Use the Image carousel pictures to teach *forest, waterfall, field, fruit farm, tractor, building, bus stop, shopping centre, street.* Ask *Where can you catch a bus?* (a bus stop) *Where can you see sheep and cows?* (in a field, on a farm) *Are we in the school playground?* (No, we're in a building.) *What is Niagara Falls* (or the name of a waterfall known to your class)*?* (a waterfall)
- Learners look at Activity A. Point to the example, and say *You can see a big forest in the countryside.* Learners work in pairs to write the other eight phrases in the correct boxes. Check answers in open class.

Answers

City – a tall building, a bus stop, a shopping centre, a busy street
Countryside – a beautiful waterfall, a green field, a little farm, an old tractor

Extension

Learners play a drawing game in groups of four (two teams of two). They have a maximum of 30 seconds to draw a picture of one of the words from Activity A, or elsewhere in the story. Their team members must guess the word. Then it's the other team's turn. Each correct guess wins one point. The team with the most points wins.

B Put the sentences in order.

- Learners read the sentences. Ask *What happens first in the story?* (Tom climbed the tallest tree in the forest.) Ask *Then what happened?* In pairs, they write 2–7 in the other boxes to show their order in the story.
- Pairs read out the sentences in the correct order.
- Ask *Can we really buy tomangoes in shops?* (no)

Answers

2 Tom heard a fruit bat in the tree.
3 Tom saw some strange red fruit.
4 Tom ate the strange fruit.
5 Tom put some fruit in his bag.
6 Tom gave the fruit to his father.
7 Tom's father planted the fruit.

Extension

In pairs or small groups, learners look back at the story and find four or five more things that happened, e.g. *Tom looked at the sea. Tom went up the hill. Tom ate three of the strange fruits. Tom ran home. People came to buy the tomangoes.* They write four or five additional sentences in their notebooks.
Ask for their suggestions and write some of them on the board. The class look at the numbered sentences in Activity B and tell you which number comes before each sentence on the board, e.g. *Tom looked at the sea* comes before number 3.

C Read and write *right* or *wrong*.

- Say *Tom is a boy. Is that right or wrong?* (right) *Tom lived in a city. Is that right or wrong?* (wrong) Look at the example. Say *Tom found a red bird in a tall tree. Is that right or wrong?* (wrong) Ask *What did Tom find in the tree?* (a fruit bat and tomangoes)
- Learners read the sentences and write *right* or *wrong*. They check their answers in pairs and by looking in the story text if necessary. Check answers in open class, encouraging learners to correct the wrong sentences, e.g. *Tom's parents were farmers.*

Answers

2 wrong **3** right **4** right **5** wrong **6** right

D What do you want to do one day? Tell a friend and write.

- Remind learners of the value discussion when they first read the story (see above) or discuss the value now for the first time.
- Ask *What did Tom want to do one day?* (go to different countries, see waterfalls, etc.)
- Ask two or three learners in open class *What do you want to do one day? Do you want to have adventures like Tom? Or do you want to be a doctor? A film star? A farmer?*
- Learners then talk in groups about what they want to do one day. Allow some discussion in L1 if necessary, but walk around and help with vocabulary.
- Read Tom's speech bubble together. Say *Now you write about hopes and dreams for your future.* Help with vocabulary if necessary.
- Learners compare their sentences with a partner.

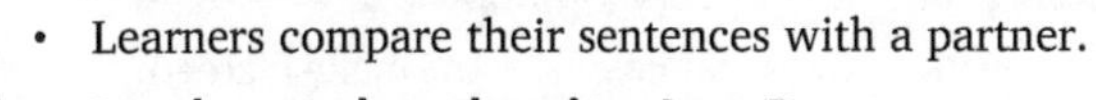

E Look, read and write *A* or *B*.

- Learners look at the pictures. Ask *Where's Tom now?* (at the top of the tree) Say *In the story, Tom could see lots of things from the top of the tree. What could he see?* (the hills, the farm, etc.)

- Ask *Can you climb trees now? Could you climb trees when you were a baby? Can you ride a bike now? Could you ride a bike when you were five?* If necessary, explain that *could* is the past form of *can*.
- Learners read the instruction, then look at pictures A and B and at the example. Ask *Why is the answer A?* (Because in picture A, Tom could see the river.) In pairs, learners write A or B next to sentences 2–6.
- Check the answers in open class.

Answers
2 A **3** B **4** B **5** A **6** A

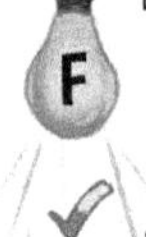

F Find the picture on page 36. Listen, colour and write.

- Learners look at the second picture on page 36. In small groups, learners find as many things that begin with the letter *c* as they can. Ask for two in open class, e.g. *clock, chair*. Ask *Who can see more than five? More than eight? More than ten?*
- Learners take turns to suggest answers. Write all the words on the board: *cage, camera, canoe, carpet, CDs, chair, child, clock, clothes, cloud, comics, computer, countryside, cow, cup, cupboard, curtains.*

17

- Check learners have crayons or colouring pencils. Tell learners they will listen to five conversations and must colour four things in this picture, as well as write one word. Play the audio twice.
- Give learners time to finish colouring their pictures and to show them to each other.
- Ask *What did you colour? What colour is it?*

Answers

laptop – green
cup on desk – pink
comic on bed – purple
T-shirt Tom is wearing – orange
'Farm' should be written on the cupboard under 'Top'.

Tapescript:

Girl: Is this where Tom sleeps?
Man: In the farmhouse … yes! Let's colour this picture now.
Girl: OK. There's a cloud in the sky. Can I colour that first?
Man: Yes. Colour it yellow, please.
Girl: All right.

Can you see the yellow cloud? This is an example. Now you listen and colour and write.

1 **Man:** Colour Tom's laptop, now.
Girl: OK. What colour? Can I make it green?
Man: Yes, that's a good idea.
Girl: Thanks.

2 **Girl:** I like Tom's desk. That's the place where Tom sits and works, I think.
Man: Yes! Colour the cup that's on his desk. You choose the colour for that.
Girl: Shall I colour it pink?
Man: All right.
Girl: Is there a drink in it?
Man: I don't know! I can't see!

3 **Man:** Now colour a comic.
Girl: The one on the floor?
Man: No. The one on his bed.
Girl: OK. Can I make it purple?
Man: Yes, you can.

4 **Girl:** What about the T-shirt that Tom's wearing?
Man: Would you like to colour that now?
Girl: Yes, please. Can I colour it brown?
Man: Umm … let's make it orange.
Girl: All right. I like that colour, too.

5 **Man:** And now I'd like you to write something.
Girl: On the front of Tom's cupboard?
Man: Yes. Under the word 'Top', write 'Farm'.
Girl: OK. Is that the name of their farm, then?
Man: That's right! Thank you.

G Complete the sentences with a word from the box.

- Say *Look at the picture. This is Julia. What's she doing?* Learners suggest ideas.
- Read the instruction and the example aloud. Ask *What did Julia take to the forest?* (a book) Write on the board *take → took*. Say *'Took' is the past tense of 'take'.*
- Check that learners understand that they must change the form of the words in the box, and that they know all the irregular past forms. If necessary, go back through the story to identify the past forms.
- Say *Now you complete the sentences using the words from the box.* Learners choose and write the words in the past simple. Check answers in open class.

Answers
2 put **3** sang **4** grew **5** ate

H Listen and draw lines.

- Ask *How many people are in this picture?* (nine) *What are they doing?* (standing, talking, buying, carrying a bag, smiling, listening, sitting, picking a tomango, walking, waving, working, etc.) Write these verbs on the board. Different learners mime a verb that's on the board. Others guess which one they're miming.
- Ask *How many names can you see outside the picture?* (seven) *Why are these people on Tom's farm?* (They want to buy tomangoes or they are working on the farm.)

18

- Say *Listen to Tom. He's talking to his grandmother about five of these people. What are their names? Draw lines.* Play the audio twice. Learners listen and draw lines from the names to the people in the picture.
- Pairs compare their answers. Then check in open class. Ask *Who's this? What's he/she doing? What's he/ she wearing?*

Answers

Clare – woman with a scarf on her head
Paul – man with a beard and a motorbike
Fred – boy listening to music, sitting on grass
Sally – young woman holding brown bag, wearing yellow T-shirt
Charlie – man with a bag of fruit, standing next to the sheep

Tapescript:

Tom: Lots of people who live in the city came to buy our fruit on Saturday! Look at this picture!
Gran: Oh yes!
Tom: I know some of them now. There's Vicky. Look! She's waving.
Gran: Do you mean the girl in the red sweater?
Tom: Yes. Her parents came last weekend, too. Her family loves our fruit.
Gran: I'm not surprised! So do I!

Can you see the line? This is an example. Now you listen and draw lines.

1 **Tom:** Clare was there, too. She's carrying some fruit back to her car.
Gran: Do you mean the woman with the scarf on her head?
Tom: That's right.
Gran: She looks very happy!

2 **Gran:** Who's the man with the beard?
Tom: His name's Paul. He's a pop star! His motorbike is so cool!
Gran: Does he always ride that to the farm?
Tom: Yes.

3 **Gran:** What about the boy that's listening to music?
Tom: The one who's sitting on the grass?
Gran: That's right.
Tom: Oh, that's Fred. He thinks shopping is really boring!

4 **Tom:** And there's Sally. She's in this picture, too. Can you see her?
Gran: No ... Which one's she?
Tom: She's holding a brown paper bag.
Gran: Oh ... the person in the yellow T-shirt!
Tom: Yes. She enjoys helping us.

5 **Gran:** Who's that? The man who bought lots of fruit?
Tom: He's called Charlie. He wants to be a farmer one day!
Gran: Well, I can see he likes sheep.
Tom: Yes! Me too, but they never stop eating!
Gran: Well, thanks for showing me your picture.

Test tip: MOVERS
Listening (Part 1)

✔ Learners will see four names above the picture and three names below it. They need to draw lines between five of the names to people in the picture (one is given as an example). Make sure learners know the 14 Movers names and whether they are used to name boys/men, girls/women or for either gender.

➜ Teach learners the complete list of Starters and Movers names and use them frequently in any other activities you might add to lessons.
Movers names:
For boys: Fred, Jack, Jim, Paul, Peter
For girls: Clare, Daisy, Jane, Julia, Lily, Mary, Sally, Vicky, Zoe
For boys or girls: Charlie

I

Find and write the words.

- Read the poem aloud. Ask for suggestions to complete the gaps (*trees, cakes, riding/reading/travelling/sitting, CDs, hats, walking/skiing/playing/jumping*). Write suggestions on the board.
- Say *Now look at the wordsnake in the leaf. Draw circles around the words.* Check the words in open class.
- Learners work in pairs to complete the poem, using the words they found.
- Ask learners to read out different lines of the poem with the words included. They can add actions to make this more fun, e.g. for *climbing very tall trees*, learners mime climbing with their hands and arms.
- Ask *Which of these things do you like doing?* Learners vote for their favourite activity.
- In pairs, learners practise Part 4 of the Speaking Test, asking and answering these questions: *What do you love doing? What do you like playing? What do you love eating? What do you like wearing?* Walk around and help with vocabulary if necessary.
- Learners talk about their own or their partner's answers in open class, e.g. *I love / (Mario) loves playing football. (Sofia) loves eating pasta.*

Answers

2 cakes **3** travelling **4** CDs **5** hats **6** playing

Test tip: MOVERS
Speaking (Part 4)

✔ Learners will be asked one *Tell me about ...* question. They should try to say three things.

➜ Help learners to prepare for this by asking questions about people in pictures or about their real-life situations. Learners could create and read out fact files about themselves / people they know, their hobbies, etc.: *My family is great. My dad drives a bus and my mum is a nurse. We live in a small flat. I love basketball. I'm good at throwing. I like playing with my friends.*

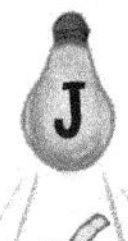

Let's talk about free time. Ask and answer questions with friends. Complete the table.

- Learners read the questions in the four speech bubbles. Encourage them to ask you the questions. Give true or funny answers, e.g. *I play tennis after school with my pet giraffe.* Learners might like to ask more questions, e.g. *How old is your pet giraffe? Who wins?*
- Say *Now it's your turn. Ask and answer the questions.* Learners talk about the questions in pairs.
- Then learners find a new partner and repeat the procedure.

Extension

Tell learners to say three things to the class about one of their partners, based on the questions they asked. Ask them to say two things that are true and one thing that is false. The class guesses which information is false.

Let's have fun!

Design a farm.

Ask *What can you see on a farm?* Learners suggest ideas. Write some of their ideas on the board. Learners look at page 70. In pairs, they decide what to put in each field. Learners colour and label their picture.

Two pairs then compare their drawings. Write the following model on the board to help learners make comparisons: *In our picture there's ..., but in your picture there's ...* Give some examples: *In my picture there are two lemon trees, but in your picture there's an orange tree. In my picture the cow is near the river, but in your picture it's next to the path. In my picture there are three sheep, but in your picture there are two.*

Let's speak!

What would you like to do on Saturday? Talk to your friend.

Learners look at page 73, Activity 5. Read the conversation aloud with a learner. Ask *What would you like to do on Saturday?* Write on the board *On Saturday, I'd like to ...* Encourage learners to tell the class what they'd like to do using this structure, e.g. *On Saturday, I'd like to go shopping with my friend. On Saturday, I'd like to try ice skating. On Saturday, I'd like to buy some new CDs.* Accept any possible or impossible fun answers! Help with vocabulary if necessary.

Learners ask and answer about their plans in pairs.

They can write and illustrate one plan in their notebooks as homework.

32

 ***Let's say!***

Say *Look at page 75, Activity 5. Listen.*
Play the audio. Learners listen.
Say *Let's say /əʊ/ goat, cold, boat.* Learners repeat. Say *Tell me more English words with /əʊ/.* Learners answer (e.g. *old, tomato, throw, coat*). Learners listen again to the audio, repeating the rhyme as fast as they can.

 **Home FUN booklet**

Pages 10–11 and 24–25 food and drink, transport
Picture dictionary: food and drink, transport

Go online

to practise your English
to listen to the audio recordings
to find more FUN activities!

6 Do whales have stomach-ache?

Main topics:	health, parts of the body, animals
Story summary:	Fred talks a lot about animals. Does he stop talking when he gets ill?
Main grammar:	superlative adjectives, *have to, must*
Main vocabulary:	*arm, back* (n),*body, bottle, bounce* (v), *called, clever, cold, cough, cup, dentist, doctor, dolphin, ear, eye, face, favourite, glass, grow, head, headache, heart, horrible, hurt, ill, be interested, jellyfish, last, laugh, leg, leopard, little, lose, medicine, octopus, orange juice, penguin, polar bear, poster, scary, sea, shark, shhhh!, shoulder, sometimes, spoon, spot, stomach, stomach-ache, stop, temperature, time, tooth, toothache, wall, whale, world, younger*
Value:	Wanting to learn about the world (*"Do you know…?"*)
***Let's say!*:**	/eɪ/
Practice tasks:	Reading and Writing Part 1 (A), Listening Part 4 (E)
Test tasks:	Speaking Part 1 (H), Reading and Writing Part 6 (I)

Equipment:

- audio: Story, E
- presentation PLUS flashcards
  Go to Presentation plus to find pictures of Movers vocabulary from Unit 6. You can use the pictures to teach/review important words in this unit.
- presentation PLUS Image carousel 30–31
  (living room, animals): Storytelling, D
- Photocopy 6(a) (TB page 58) (one per learner): Storytelling Extension
- Photocopy 6(b) (TB page 59) (one per learner): Let's have fun!
- crayons / colouring pencils: Storytelling Extension, Let's have fun!

Storytelling

Before listening

With books closed …

- Introduce the topic of the story. Show learners the photograph of the living room from the Image carousel. Say *Look! Where is it?* (a living room) Ask learners about younger children. Ask *Do you have younger brothers or sisters? How are they different? Are they shorter, naughtier, quieter, louder than you?* Say *This story is about someone's younger brother. He is interested in animals.*
- Learners look at the first story picture (with or without the text) on the Image carousel or on page 44. Ask *Where is this family?* (in the living room) *Who's talking?* (the small boy / the younger brother) *What's he showing his mother?* (a picture of an octopus) *How old is he?* Learners guess.
- Look at the first story picture again. Say *Look at the boy in the green T-shirt. Is he happy?* (no) *Why?* Learners guess. (He wants his brother to be quiet.)
- Say *Now let's listen to the story. Look at page 44.*

Listening

With books open …

19

- Play the audio or read the story. Learners listen.
- Play the audio or read the story again.
- Pause after *'Yes, I know!' Mum said.* on page 45. Ask *What is the little boy's name?* (Fred) *What was the matter with Fred on Saturday?* (He had spots on his face.) *Who came to look at Fred's spots?* (Aunt Jane / the doctor) *Which animals is Fred interested in?* (parrots, pandas, polar bears, penguins, lions, leopards, rabbits, jellyfish, whales, dolphins, sharks, octopuses)
- Pause again after *'I don't know, Fred,' Aunt Jane said.* on page 46. Ask *What did Aunt Jane look at?* (Fred's spots/ ears/eyes/mouth) *Did Fred stop talking?* (no) *What did he talk about?* (octopuses, whales, dolphins, sharks)

After listening

- After listening to the whole story, ask *What did Aunt Jane want to give Fred?* (medicine) *Did Fred want to open his mouth?* (no) *What question did Aunt Jane ask?* (Do whales have stomach-ache?) *Did Fred open his mouth to answer the question?* (yes)

Value

- Ask *What is Fred interested in?* (animals) *Is it good to be interested in the world?* Learners answer in L1 if necessary. Ask *What are you interested in?* Learners suggest ideas.

Extension

Give each learner Photocopy 6(a) (TB page 58). Tell them to fold the page in three along the dotted lines so they can see only the top third and the neck and shoulders. Show them how to do this.

Make sure all learners have crayons or colouring pencils. Point to the top part of the paper and say *Let's draw funny bodies! Draw a head here.* Give learners plenty of time to do this. Say *You can draw a person's head or an animal's head or a monster's head. You choose.* Encourage learners to make their drawings funny if they wish to. Show learners how to fold the paper so they can see the bottom of the shoulders and the top of the legs. In smaller classes, say *Give your drawing to another person in the classroom now.* Learners do that and sit down again. In larger classes, learners give their picture to their neighbour.

Say *Don't look at the top part of the picture. Draw the arms, hands, stomach and top of the legs.* Point to these parts of your body when you say this. Say *You can see the top of the legs. Stop your drawing there.*
Show learners how to fold the paper so they can see only the top of the legs. Say *Now give your drawing to another person.*

Say *Don't look at the other parts of the picture. Now draw the legs and feet.*
Learners then give their picture to their partner, who opens it up. Display these funny-body drawings on a wall. Ask *Which is the funniest / scariest / most beautiful picture?*

A Read and write the correct word.

- Learners look at the pictures. Ask *What animals can you see?* (a panda, a rabbit, a lion) *What people can you see?* (a doctor, a dentist) *What can you drink from?* (a cup, a bottle)
- Read the example together. Then ask *What can you buy fruit juice in?* (a bottle)
- Learners read sentences 2–6 in pairs. They choose and write the correct word. Check answers.

Answers

2 a panda **3** a rabbit **4** a doctor **5** a lion **6** a dentist

Extension

Fast finishers can look for the words in the story and think of sentences about the story using the words, e.g. *Fred has posters of pandas, Aunt Jane is a doctor.*

B Put the sentences (2–9) in the correct box.

- Say something correct and something incorrect about yesterday, e.g. *It was Sunday yesterday. Is that right? It rained yesterday. Is that right?*
- Learners look at sentence 1 and at the number 1 in the 'wrong' box. Say *Fred liked being quiet. Is that right or wrong?* (wrong) Say *So we put number 1 in the 'wrong' box. Now put the numbers of the right sentences in the 'right' box* (hold up your book and point) *and the numbers of the wrong sentences in the 'wrong' box* (hold up your book and point).
- Learners read sentences 2–9 and write the numbers in the correct boxes. Learners then check their answers in pairs and by looking at the story again if necessary. Check in open class.
- Ask *Which sentences are wrong?* (1, 4, 5, 6, 8) *Why is sentence 1 wrong?* (Because Fred never stopped talking.) Ask *Do you like being quiet?* Learners share their ideas.

Answers

right: 2, 3, 7, 9 **wrong:** 1, 4, 5, 6, 8

Extension

Learners discuss the wrong sentences in pairs or small groups, explaining why they are incorrect. They can refer back to the story.

C What's different? Circle the wrong words. Write the right words.

- Remind learners of the value discussion when they first read the story (see above) or discuss the value now for the first time.
- Say *Tell me more about Fred. What does he like doing? What's he interested in? What posters has he got? What are his favourite animals?* Learners answer from memory.
- Say *Look at the text.* Read the example together. Ask *Why does 'answers' have a circle around it?* (It's wrong, Fred asks questions about animals.) Ask *Can you see 'asks'?*
- Say *There are some more mistakes. Read and draw circles around the words that are wrong. Write the correct words above them.*
- In pairs, learners circle and correct the other wrong words. They can check in the story.

Answers

parents→ parrots
pancakes→ pandas
libraries→ lions
rainbows→ rabbits
apartments→ animals
sky→ sea
dolls→ dolphins
showers→ sharks
basement→ bedroom

D Talk with a friend and complete the sentences.

- Learners look at the animals on the Image carousel. In pairs, they list them according to size (e.g. rabbit, octopus, leopard, lion, dolphin, panda, whale). Ask *Is a rabbit smaller than a lion?* (yes) *Is a dolphin smaller than a whale?* (yes)
- Show a picture of a rabbit, a dolphin and a whale. Say *The rabbit is the smallest animal. A dolphin and a whale are bigger than a rabbit.* Write on the board *The rabbit is the smallest animal.* You may like to write *the* and *-est* in a different colour to make the structure stand out. Avoid writing *biggest* at this stage as that has an irregular spelling.

- Say *I think the rabbit is the most beautiful, too!* Write that sentence on the board, underlining or showing *the* and *most* in a different colour. Say *We don't add '-est' to beautiful. We use 'most'.*
- Summarise. Tell learners we can add *-est* to short adjectives of one syllable or two syllables ending in *-y* (in which case the *y* changes to *i*). Explain we use the word *most* with adjectives of two or more syllables. Use L1 if necessary.
- Ask learners to look at the sentences again. Ask *Which word always comes before the '-est' word or 'most'?* (the)
- Learners look at the animals on the Image carousel again. Ask *Which is the longest / most beautiful animal here?* Accept various answers.
- Learners look at Activity D. Read the examples. Explain that they must choose words from the box to make sentences 3–7 and that they may need to add *-est* to some of the words in the box. Explain that they do not need to use all the adjectives in the box. Learners say the complete sentences with a partner. When they finish, ask each pair to say a sentence for the class.
- Learners find and circle the three *-est* words in the story. Ask *What are they?* (biggest, cleverest, nicest)

Extension

Write the following on the board for learners to copy:
the oldest/tallest/quietest person in my family
the biggest/smallest/coldest room in my house/flat
the most interesting story in this book
They write six sentences using these phrases and illustrate their ideas if they wish, e.g. *The oldest person in my family is my grandma.*

E Listen and tick (✔) the box.

- Learners look at the 12 pictures. Review/Teach the vocabulary. Say *Look at question 1. Where are the spots?* (on the neck, on the leg, on the arm) *Look at question 2. What hurts?* (his back, his shoulder, his foot) *Look at question 3. What's the matter?* (a toothache, a stomach-ache, a headache) *Look at question 4. What's the matter in these pictures?* (a cough, tired, a cold)
- 20 Say *Listen to some people talking about Fred. What's the matter with Fred now? Read the questions and tick the boxes.* Play the audio twice.
- Check answers in open class.
- Write on the board *Fred must stay at home today.* Ask *Can he go out?* (no) *No, he must stay at home. 'Must' is like 'has to'. We can say 'he must stay' or 'he has to stay'.* Write *Fred has to stay at home* on the board.

Answers

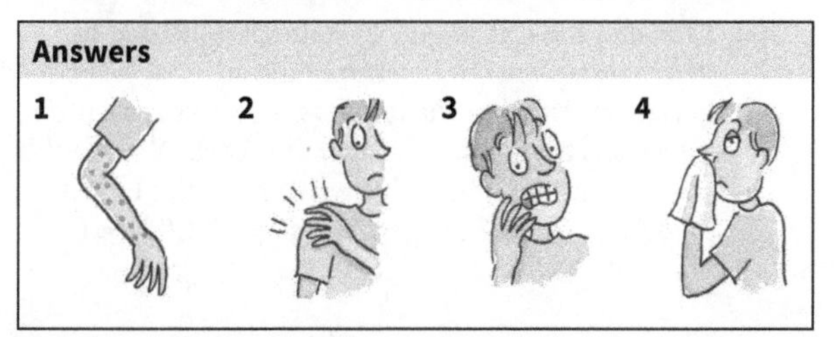

Tapescript:

1 Where are Fred's spots?

Doctor: Now, Fred. Tell me about these spots. Where are they? I can't see any on your neck.
Fred: The biggest spots are on my arms, Doctor. Look!
Doctor: OK. And have you got any spots on your legs?
Fred: No, I haven't.

2 What hurts?

Mum: Why are you walking like that, Fred? Is your foot hurting?
Fred: No. I played football. I played football with the tallest and strongest boys in the school …
Mum: And did you hurt your back?
Fred: No, Mum. But my shoulder hurts. Ouch ...

3 What's the matter with Fred now?

Dad: Hello! I've got a bad headache. Where's Fred?
Mum: He's in bed.
Dad: Oh! Why? Has he got stomach-ache?
Mum: No. He needs to see a dentist! He's got toothache.

4 Why isn't Fred at school today?

Man: Where's Fred? Has he got a cough again?
Girl: No, Mr Nick. But his mum says he can't come to school today.
Man: Oh dear! Why? Is he tired?
Girl: No. He's got a cold. That's all. Don't worry!

Test tip: MOVERS
Listening (Part 4)

✔ Learners listen to a conversation and choose the correct picture (of three) that shows the answer to a question. Before doing this task, train learners to carefully look at all three pictures and to look for differences between them.

➜ Train learners to quickly spot the difference in picture sets. Give learners sets of three pictures, e.g. three different animals, activities, items of clothing, and ask them to say what they see in each set, e.g. *This is a bat, a snail and a parrot. This man's working on a computer here, watching TV here, and looking at a tablet here. This girl's wearing jeans here, shorts here, and a skirt here.*

Read and draw lines to make sentences.

- Learners find the part of the story where Aunt Jane tells Fred he needs some medicine (page 46). Read the complete paragraph with the class. Write the last part on the board: *...you mustn't go shopping today. You can go to the shopping centre to get your book and DVD on Monday. OK?*
- Ask *Why did Fred want to go to the shopping centre?* (He wanted to get a book and a DVD.) Underline the phrase *to get your book* on the board. Point to the example.
- Say *These words answer the question 'Why?'* Write *Why?* before the phrase. Say *I'm going to the café now ... Why? ... to buy the biggest burger in town!*
- Learners draw lines to make sentences. Check answers.

Answers
2 buy some medicine. **3** look at his spots. **4** ask her to come. **5** ask about his English lesson. **6** practise skateboarding.

Let's talk about Fred's brother. Ask and answer with a friend. Complete the notes.

- With books closed, show learners a picture of a girl. Write the following prompts on the board *What's her name? What does she like ... -ing?*
- Learners talk in pairs and invent information about the girl. Encourage them to think of some funny answers, e.g. *Her name is ... Ziggy! She likes making ... ice-cream soup, swimming with ... sharks and looking for ... bats!*
- Learners now look at the picture in Activity G. Ask *Who's this?* (Fred's brother) Say *Read the questions. Ask and answer more questions.* In small groups, learners read and answer the questions. Walk around and help with any problems, encouraging learners to be imaginative. Learners agree on and write their answers on the form.

Find six differences. Point and say.

- Learners look at the pictures. Say *Some things in the two pictures are different. Here there's a whale, but here there's a dolphin.*
- Say *In this picture, there are four people, but in that picture there are ...?* (six people) Write these models on the board: *Here there's a ..., but here there's a ... In this picture there are ..., but in that picture there are ...*
- In pairs or small groups, learners find four more differences by pointing or using single words. They then think how to describe the differences in complete sentences using the models on the board. Groups take turns to say one difference each.

Suggested answers
There is a picture of a whale/dolphin on the wall. There are four/six people. A girl/boy is standing on the chair. The dog has / doesn't have spots. The biggest book on the table is red/blue. The woman isn't/is wearing glasses.

Look at picture 2 in H. Read and write.

- Learners read the instruction. Ask *Which picture do you need?* (picture 2) Point to the second picture in Activity H. Read the examples together. Ask *Can you find the boy in jeans and the dog on the grass?* Say *Now you write the answers.* Learners complete the rest of the activity.

Suggested answers
1 red table **2** glasses / a red top / a white T-shirt **3** reading (a (big) book (about boats)) **4** a dolphin **Suggested answers for 5 and 6:** This is a library. Some children are reading. There are some toys by the window. There are lots of books in the bookcase. The man has grey hair. The walls are yellow. One person is sitting on a grey chair. The floor is blue. The people are here because they like reading.

Test tip: MOVERS *Reading and Writing (Part 6)*
✔ Learners need to add two complete sentences about the picture. They can write about what they can actually see in the picture or what they imagine is happening. ➜ Using any picture in the book, encourage learners to write about it using simple sentences first. To get a higher mark, when learners are feeling more confident, train them to try writing compound sentences using linking words (*and, but, or, because*) or relative pronouns (*who, that, which*).

Let's have fun!

Write questions for an animal quiz.

Put learners into groups of three or four. Give each group Photocopy 6(b) (TB page 59). Read sentence number 1 together. Ask *What is it?* (a lion) Say *Draw a lion.* Say *Now you write animal quiz questions.*

Walk around and choose about 12 questions for learners to read aloud for the whole class to answer. Some answers could be used twice, for different questions, e.g. *This animal is big and it can hop really quickly. This animal is big and brown or grey and has a very long tail.* (a kangaroo)

Learners look at page 70, Activity 6. Read the instructions and the example aloud. Say *Write more questions. Find out the answers.* Learners research questions and answers for homework. You could provide more support by writing on the board *Smallest? Tallest? Longest? Strongest? Cleverest? Fastest?*

Let's speak!

What's the matter? Ask and answer.

Learners look at page 73, Activity 6. Read the speech bubbles together. Ask *What's the matter with the boy?* (His foot hurts.) Mime a headache. Encourage learners to ask you *What's the matter?* (I've got a headache. / My head hurts.) Repeat with other parts of the body.

Ask learners to role play the conversation in pairs. Encourage them to add other phrases, such as *Oh dear! Oh no! Are you OK? Do you want some water? Do you want to sit down?*

33

Let's say!

Say *Look at page 75, Activity 6. Listen.*
Play the audio. Learners listen.
Say *Let's say /eɪ/ play, game, dangerous, whale, day.*
Learners repeat. Say *Tell me more English words with /eɪ/.* Learners answer (e.g. *say, ache, lake, take*). Learners listen again to the audio, repeating the rhyme as fast as they can.

Home FUN booklet

Pages 4–5 and 12–13 the body and face, health
Picture dictionary: body and face, health

Go online

to practise your English
to listen to the audio recordings
to find more FUN activities!

7

The grey cloud

Main topics:	nature, feelings, weather
Story summary:	Aunt Clare tells a story on a boring train ride. The story is about a sad, grey cloud, and a girl who helps him.
Main grammar:	comparative adverbs and adjectives: *bad, worse, worst; good, better, best*
Main vocabulary:	*above, All right!, alone, angry, apartment, appear, aunt, behind, boring, cloud, coat, colour* (n), *cry* (v), *dance, different, fall, feel, feet, flower, grey, ground, happy, high, home, huge, ice, light, jump (up), moon, neck, often, Oh dear!, rainbow, really, ride* (n), *rock, roof, roof garden, sad, skip, slowly, snow, station, story, strong, sun, understand, wave* (v), *weak, week, wet, wind* (n)
Value:	Making others feel happier (*"That's better!"*)
***Let's say!*:**	/aʊ/
Practice tasks:	Listening Part 2 (E), Speaking Part 2 (G)
Test tasks:	Reading and Writing Part 5 (F), Reading and Writing Part 6 (G)

Equipment:

- audio: Story, E, H, I
- presentation PLUS flashcards
  Go to Presentation plus to find pictures of Movers vocabulary from Unit 7. You can use the pictures to teach/review important words in this unit.
- presentation PLUS Image carousel 32–36
  (five pictures of clouds): Storytelling, Let's have fun!
- Photocopy 7 (TB page 60) (one per learner): Let's have fun!
- crayons / colouring pencils: D Extension, Let's have fun!
- optional: card, glue, grey paint, cotton wool, wire coat hangers, string or wool: Let's have fun!

Storytelling

Before listening

With books closed …

- Introduce the topic of the story. Show learners the weather/cloud photographs from the Image carousel. Review/Teach *rainy, windy, cloud/cloudy, ice, rainbow* and *sunny*. Say *This story is about a cloud.*
- Ask learners about the weather: *What's the weather like today? Can you see any clouds in the sky? What colour are they? Did it rain this week? Did it snow?*
- Learners look at the first story picture from the Image carousel (with or without the text) or on page 52. Ask *What can you see?* (countryside, a hill, trees, grey sky, a train) *Where is it?* Learners guess. *What's the weather like?* (windy, rainy, cloudy) *Can you see a train?* (yes)
- Say *Now let's listen to the story. Look at page 52.*

Listening

With books open …

21

Play the audio or read the story. Learners listen.

Play the audio or read the story again.

- Pause after *Lily often got angry AND sad then, too.* on page 52. Ask *Why does the cloud get angry?* (Because the wind is too strong, because it is alone.) *What colour is the cloud when it's angry?* (grey) *What happens when the cloud is sad?* (It rains.)
- Pause again after *She climbed up the stairs to the roof garden.* on page 53. Ask *What happens when the cloud feels frightened?* (It snows.) *Why does Lily often get angry in the snow?* (Because walking in the snow is dangerous.) *What happens to the weather from Monday to Thursday?* (The weather gets worse.)
- Pause again after *… dance in the wind.* on page 54. Ask *What does Lily do to help the cloud?* (She skips and dances.)
- At the end of the story, ask *Is the cloud happy now?* (yes) *Is the cloud happy all the time?* (no) *Why does Aunt Clare say 'Pick up your bag!'?* (They are at the station.)

After listening

- Ask *What do you think about the story? What's your favourite part? Which is your favourite picture?* Learners suggest ideas.

Value

- Ask *What does Lily do to make the cloud happy?* (She dances, skips and climbs.) *What do you do when you are sad or frightened?*
- Ask *Are you happy all the time? Why not?* Learners answer in L1 if necessary. *What do you do when you aren't happy? Who do you talk to? What does your friend do when you aren't happy?* Learners suggest ideas.

A Find the words in the story. Read and complete.

- With books closed, check understanding of *boring* and *exciting*. Ask *What's boring – a trip to the supermarket or a trip to a funfair? What's exciting – a holiday or going to bed at seven o'clock?* Ask *What's the opposite of 'boring'?* (exciting)
- Check understanding of *better* and *worse* by talking about three children: Zoe, Mark and Lily. Say *Mark got five for his homework. Lily got three. Is his homework better* (thumbs up) *or worse* (thumbs down) *than Lily's?* (better) *Zoe got ten for her homework. Is Mark's homework better or worse than Zoe's?* (worse)
- Say *Now let's find more words from the story.* Learners open their books at page 56. Read the example in Activity A together. Ask *Which page is the answer on?* (page 52) *How many letters are there in the answer?* (six letters)
- In pairs, learners find the rest of the words from the story, underline them and complete the answers. Check answers in open class.
- Review the words one more time. Ask about them in a different order than they appear, e.g. *What can you skate on?* (ice) *What is the opposite of 'strong'?* (weak) etc.

Answers

2 worse **3** cried **4** changed **5** ice **6** weak

B Read and circle the correct answer.

- Practise the days of the week again. Ask *What day is it today?* Learners answer. *Help me remember the days of the week. Monday, Tuesday …* (Wednesday) *Thursday, Friday …* (Saturday) *Sunday.* Ask *Which day comes after Sunday?* (Monday) *Which day comes after Thursday?* (Friday) *Which day comes before Tuesday?* (Monday) *Which day comes before Thursday?* (Wednesday) Learners can form similar questions to ask their partner or the class.
- Read the instruction and the example. Ask *When did it get colder?* (When the cloud felt frightened.) Ask *Which words do you draw a circle around?* (the correct ones) In pairs, learners circle the correct answers. Check answers in open class, prompting learners to read the full sentence out loud.

Answers

2 dangerous **3** Thursday **4** roof garden **5** rain
6 rock

- Check understanding of the vocabulary with more questions, e.g. *Which sports are dangerous? Have you got a balcony at your house? Are you frightened of spiders/sharks/monsters?*

C What is the happiest answer? Tick (✔) the correct answer.

- Remind learners of the value discussion when they first read the story (see above) or discuss the value now for the first time.
- Say *Do you remember the story? What happened?* Learners summarise the story. Ask learners, in L1 if necessary, *What's the message of the story? What does Aunt Clare say at the end?* (We can't always feel happy, but skipping, dancing and climbing and laughing and playing with really good friends can always help us feel better.)
- Ask *How can you ask if someone feels happier?* (Are you happier now? Do you feel better or worse now? Are you feeling better?)
- Say *Read the speech bubbles and tick the happiest answer.* In pairs, learners read, decide and tick.

Answer

B I'm much better now, thanks.

- Ask *What can you say to a friend who is feeling sad or worried?* Write suggestions on the board, e.g. *What's the matter? Come on! Let's …, Don't worry!, We can …* In small groups, learners practise short role plays using the language on the board about being sad and helping friends feel better. Choose a few groups to perform for the rest of the class.

Extension

In groups, learners recreate a scene from the story through mime. Other classmates guess the scene and describe what is happening: *The aunt and the girl are sitting on the train. Lily is climbing on the roof. The cloud is crying,* etc.

D Choose and write *bad*, *worse* or *worst*.

- Learners look at the pictures. Check understanding of the vocabulary. Point to the weather pictures and ask *What's the weather like here? And here? And here?* Ask similar questions about the pictures for *hungry, tired* and *frightened.* Review/Teach *It's not working* and ask about the tablet, TV and phone. Ask *Is it worse when you don't have chocolate, water or fruit?*
- Learners work in pairs, talk about what's bad, worse or worst in each set and write *bad, worse* and *worst* under their chosen pictures. Make sure learners understand that there are no right or wrong answers. When learners have finished writing, ask two or three pairs to talk about one of their bad, worse or worst sets. Stronger learners could answer *Why?* questions to explain their choices.

Extension

Learners draw another set of three things to demonstrate *bad*, *worse* and *worst*. They could be foods, animals, school subjects, activities, etc. Then in groups they talk about which things are bad, worse and worst.

Listen and write.

- Learners look at the picture of the girl. Ask *Who is this?* (Lily) *Where is she?* (in her bedroom) *What's she doing?* (listening to music / thinking / sitting on her bed, etc.)
- Ask *How old is Lily?* Learners read the example on the form to find her age (ten). Before listening, ask learners to guess the answers for 2–6. Ask *What's her favourite hobby? Guess! What's her favourite food? Guess!* etc. Learners suggest ideas.

22

- Play the audio twice. Learners listen and complete the information.
- Learners compare their answers in pairs. Play the audio again if necessary. Check answers in open class.

Answers

2 music **3** coffee **4** countryside **5** raining **6** Pat

Extension

Learners answer the same questions about themselves. Ask *How are you and Lily different?*

Tapescript:

Boy:	Hi! My name's Matt. I've got to ask some of the kids in our school some questions for my homework. Is that OK?
Girl:	Yes!
Boy:	Great! Thanks. What's your name?
Girl:	Lily.
Boy:	Cool name! How old are you, Lily?
Girl:	That's a funny question because yesterday I was nine years old, but today, I'm ten!
Boy:	And what do you like doing best?
Girl:	Oh … I like listening to music!
Boy:	Right! What's your favourite food?
Girl:	I love coffee cake!
Boy:	So do I! Do you go on holiday sometimes?
Girl:	Sometimes …
Boy:	Well, what's the best place for a holiday?
Girl:	Oh ... I love being in the countryside.
Boy:	OK. What kind of weather is the worst for you?
Girl:	Oh ... when it's raining. Sunny weather is the best.
Boy:	Thanks. And what's your best friend's name?
Girl:	He's called Pat. He's lots of fun. You spell his name P-A-T.
Boy:	OK. Thanks a lot for answering my questions.

Test tip: MOVERS
Listening (Part 2)

✔ Learners may have to write a name of a school, street, town or person on their form. The name is usually less than six letters long. If the word isn't on the Starters or Movers word list, it is usually spelled out.

➜ Give learners practice in both spelling and writing names correctly. Learners can make up names of an imaginary friend, the road they live in and the school they go to and write these down secretly. They then spell these names out and their partner writes them down. Learners compare spellings.

Look at the pictures and read the story. Write 1, 2 or 3 words to complete the sentences.

- Learners look at the pictures and the story title. Ask *Who can you see in the picture?* (Charlie and Pat) *How do they feel?* (happy) Say *Read the instructions. How many words do you need to write?* (1, 2 or 3) *Can you write only one word?* (yes) *Can you write four words?* (no)
- Learners read the first part of the story and look at the examples. Ask *Where do Pat and Charlie live?* (in a village) Say *Find that sentence in the story.* Learners find and underline the information. Ask *When did Pat phone Charlie?* (last Saturday) Learners underline that information in the story, too. Say *Now you complete sentences 1 to 7.* Learners work in pairs or individually to find the right words in the story and write them in the gaps. Walk around and help as necessary. Check answers in open class.

Answers

1 the city **2** to help **3** park **4** (huge) pool
5 a (funny) text **6** his mum **7** (chocolate) pancakes

Test tip: MOVERS
Reading and Writing (Part 5)

✔ Structures in the story text and in the sentences to be completed might be different. However, the words that learners need to write should be copied from the story text. Learners will not need to change these to complete their answers.

➜ Give learners practice in transforming sentences. For example: *Last Wednesday, Paul went roller skating with his friends. / Paul went roller skating with his friends on Wednesday. Julia enjoyed going to the funfair on Saturday afternoon. / On Saturday afternoon, Julia had fun at the funfair.*

Look and read and write.

- Make a binocular shape by forming your hands into two circles. Hold them to your eyes and look towards the classroom window. Say *I can see three enormous trees! I can see a green car and a big blue bus! There's a woman walking. She's wearing a grey sweater.* Make clear from your tone that learners don't really have to see what they describe. Gesture for learners to make binoculars with their hands, too. Ask *What can you see?* Learners say sentences. Help with vocabulary as needed.

- Learners look at the picture in Activity G. Ask *What can you see in the picture?* Learners suggest answers. Encourage lots of answers by asking *What are they doing? What are they wearing? What colour is it / are they? What's the weather like? Can you see any animals? Where? What do they look like?*
- Learners look at the examples. Say *You can write more than one word in your answers for 1 to 4. Now complete the sentences, answer the questions and write two sentences about the story.* Learners work on their own. Ask different learners for their answers, reminding the class that there is often more than one way to complete the sentences and answer the questions.
- Check answers in open class.

Suggested answers

1 a hat, a scarf, a brown coat, ice skates
2 mountains/hills
3 sunny/cold
4 on a/the rock / under a tree
5 and **6**: The children are having fun. They are good at ice skating. I can see a town. I can see some trees.

Test tip: MOVERS
Reading and Writing (Part 6) and Speaking (Part 2)

✔ Learners need to use their imagination a little in these two tasks as both use pictures. In Reading and Writing Part 6, learners write sentences, and in Speaking Part 2, they tell the story. Encourage learners to imagine information that they can't necessarily 'see' in the pictures.

➜ Choose any picture at different points in a lesson and ask learners in groups to use their imagination to tell you more about the picture. Learners usually really enjoy this, so accept all answers. You can ask questions to prompt them if they find this difficult, e.g. *What do you think is in that boy's bag? Who lives in that house? What's behind that mountain? What is that girl's favourite hobby?*

H Where are these people? Listen and tick (✔) three places.

- Before listening, ask *Can you name all these places?* (a pool, some mountains, a cinema, a river/bridge, a funfair, the countryside). Put learners into small groups. Say *Where can I say 'I love swimming here'?* (at the pool) *What can you say at the other places?* Learners think of one thing they might say in each place. Walk around and help with vocabulary if necessary.

23

- Say *Now listen. Where are these three people? Tick the places.* Play the audio twice. Learners listen and tick.
- After listening, learners compare answers with a partner. Play the audio again, pausing after each number to ask *Where are they?* (cinema, mountains, pool)

Answers

1 C **2** F **3** A

Tapescript:

1	**Girl:**	Here's my seat. This is exciting. It's a really cool movie about a trip along a river, and my two favourite film stars are in it.
2	**Woman:**	Wow! I'm tired, but it's fantastic to be at the top. Look at all the countryside below us! But oh dear ... it's starting to rain.
3	**Man:**	Be careful. There are lots of people in the water today! And don't run around the outside. When people do that, they sometimes fall in!

I Listen and say the poem.

24

- Learners look at the poem. Review/Teach *high*, then say *This is a poem about something high. What is it? Listen and watch.* Play the audio and demonstrate the following actions for learners to follow.

I'm high and I'm white	(Look up)
But I am not a kite.	(Mime pulling on a string)
You can climb up me.	(Mime climbing with hands)
But I am not a tree.	(Hold arms in circle above head)
Clouds sit on my shoulders.	(Touch both shoulders)
My ground grows small flowers.	(Mime flowers blooming by opening)
My top touches the sky.	(Point to the sky)
Can you do that? Try!	(Nod)

- Ask *What am I?* (a mountain) *Am I a tree?* (no) *Am I a kite?* (no) *What's on my shoulders?* (clouds)
- Say *Stand up.* Play the audio again. Learners say the poem together with the actions.

7 *Let's have fun!*

Make a cloud information mobile.

Say *Look at page 71. Complete the information.* Learners can either complete the gaps using language clues (e.g. an *-ing* form is needed for the third gap) or by researching the different cloud types online or in books. Check answers in open class.

Answers

storms raining sunny fog

Point to the picture of the mobile. Show learners how to make a cloud mobile with string or wool, pictures of clouds and a coat hanger. The clouds can be decorated with cotton wool and grey paint. Hang the clouds from coat hangers to make mobiles.

As a follow-up, learners find out more about different kinds and shapes of clouds and the weather that might follow. Give each learner a copy of Photocopy 7 (TB page 60). Learners use it to collect information to create a cloud poster. If learners did the Let's have fun! activity using language clues, they could now look online or in books, or they can listen to you read the useful information on page 48.

Useful information about five types of clouds:

1 **Cirrus:** thin and white. These are high in the sky and have lots of ice in them. We usually see this kind of cloud before rain or snow.
2 **Cumulus:** white and round. These clouds are in the sky in sunny weather.
3 **Cumulonimbus:** tall clouds that go up in the sky. You usually see them before storms.
4 **Stratus:** low in the sky. These look like grey blankets. They change to fog when they get lower and lower in the sky.
5 **Nimbostratus:** dark clouds. You see these in the sky when it rains or snows all day.

Learners can illustrate their poster using their own drawings or images found online or in magazines. You can also show them the photographs of clouds on the Image carousel.

7 *Let's speak!*

Make a friend happier. Write a conversation and act it out.

Say *Look at page 73, Activity 7.* Read the speech bubbles together. Ask *What's the matter?* (He's really hungry.) Ask *What happens?* (The other boy gives him some of his sandwich.) As a class, brainstorm other problems (e.g. thirsty, tired, can't do homework, can't find something, too hot, too cold). Write them on the board. In small groups, learners choose problems and role play the conversation. Help with vocabulary and structures as learners suggest solutions.

Ask learners to perform their finished role plays for the class.

34

Let's say!

Say *Look at page 75, Activity 7. Listen.*
Play the audio. Learners listen.
Say *Let's say /aʊ/ cloud, flower, around, town.* Learners repeat. Say *Tell me more English words with /aʊ/.* Learners answer (e.g. *clown, house, mouse, trousers*). Learners listen again to the audio, repeating the rhyme as fast as they can.

Home FUN booklet

Pages 26–27 and 30 weather, adjectives
Picture dictionary: weather

Go online

to practise your English
to listen to the audio recordings
to find more FUN activities!

8 The fancy-dress shop

Main topics:	clothes, jobs, feelings
Story summary:	Zoe is going to a fancy-dress party. Something surprising happens when she tries on a pirate costume in the fancy-dress shop.
Main grammar:	*How about …? What about …?*
Main vocabulary:	*address, afraid, afternoon, alien, back* (prep), *beard, best, boots, carry, clown, costume, curly, dream* (v), *drip* (v), *end, fancy dress* (n, adj), *firefighter, floor, for* (prep. of time), *hair, hat, helmet, invite, jacket, kangaroo, kitten, moustache, nose, nurse, party, pirate, room, sail* (n), *ship, shirt, shop, shout, snowman, splash, text message, treasure, trousers, uniform, wave* (n), *wear*
Value:	Saying how you feel (*"This is getting scary!"*)
***Let's say!*:**	/ɜː/
Practice tasks:	Listening Part 1 (D), Reading and Writing Part 1 (E), Reading and Writing Part 6 (I), Listening Part 2 (J)
Test tasks:	Reading and Writing Part 4 (G), Speaking Part 4 (H)

Equipment:

- audio: Story, D, J
- presentation PLUS flashcards
  Go to Presentation plus to find pictures of Movers vocabulary from Unit 8. You can use the pictures to teach/review important words in this unit.
- presentation PLUS Image carousel 37–39 (three pictures of children in fancy dress): Storytelling
- Photocopy 8 (TB page 61) (one per learner): C Extension
- crayons / colouring pencils: C Extension
- a map: G

Storytelling

Before listening

With books closed …

- Introduce the topic of the story by asking about parties: *When did you go to a party? Was it good? What did you wear to the party?* Say *This story is about a girl who goes to a fancy-dress shop.* Show learners a picture from the Image carousel of someone in fancy dress. Say *Fancy dress doesn't mean dresses. It means clothes that we wear to a party when we want to look like someone or something. We call them fancy-dress clothes.* Ask *What fancy-dress clothes can you wear?* Learners suggest ideas (e.g. clothes for a clown, a doctor, to make you look like a tiger).
- Write *fancy-dress shop* on the board and say *This is where you can buy fancy-dress clothes. Let's read a story about this place.*
- Learners read the first line of the story and the text message on page 60. Ask *When is the party?* (on Thursday at three o'clock) *Where is it?* (31, Lake Road) *What must Zoe wear to the party?* (fancy dress) *Why is Jim having the party?* Learners guess.
- Learners look at the first story picture from the Image carousel (with or without the text) or on page 60. Ask *What can you see?* (a busy street) *Where are Zoe and her mum going?* (the fancy-dress shop) *What's in the window?* (clown clothes) *Does Zoe want to be a clown?* Learners guess.
- Say *Now let's listen to the story. Look at page 60.*

Listening

With books open …

25

- Play the audio or read the story. Learners listen.
- Play the audio or read the story again.
- Pause after *'Can I try it, please?' she asked the man in the shop.* on page 61. Ask *Where were Zoe and her mum?* (in the fancy-dress shop) *Which animal fancy-dress clothes were in the shop?* (panda, kangaroo, kitten) *Which clothes did Zoe like?* (the pirate's clothes)
- Pause after *But Zoe couldn't move!* on page 62. Ask *Where was Zoe?* (on a ship) *Which clothes did Zoe have on?* (trousers, shirt, boots, scarf, hat) *Was Zoe happy?* (No, she was afraid.)

After listening

- After listening to the whole story, ask *Why didn't Zoe want to wear the alien clothes?* (She didn't want to go to the moon.) *Which clothes did Zoe wear to the party?* (the kitten costume)

Value

- Ask, in L1 if necessary, *How does Zoe feel about the party at the start of the story?* (excited) *How does she feel when she's trying on the pirate clothes?* (happy) *How does she feel on the pirate ship?* (afraid, frightened) *How does she feel about the kitten fancy dress?* (happy)
- Ask *What can you say to tell someone your feelings?* (I feel … , I'm feeling …) Discuss in L1 if necessary.

A Find the words in the story and complete the sentences.

- Read the example together. Ask *Can you see the first letter of the word? How many letters are in 'wave'?* (four)
- In pairs, learners read the sentences and guess the words, but don't write them. They look in the story to find the words, underline them, then complete the words in the activity.
- Check answers. Ask different learners to read the sentences. Make sure they pronounce the new words correctly.

Answers

2 moustache **3** treasure **4** helmet **5** message

B Who said this? Read and write A, B or C.

- Learners read the instruction and the example. Ask *Why is the answer A?* (Because Zoe said this and Zoe is A.) Ask *Who is B?* (the pirate) *Who is C?* (Zoe's mum)
- In pairs, learners read sentences 2–7 and write A, B or C. If they can't remember who said each thing, they check in the story text.
- Check answers. Ask for A, B or C answers and tell different learners to read what was said in a voice that shows if it's Zoe (A), the pirate (B) or Zoe's mum (C).

Answers

2 A **3** B **4** C **5** B **6** A **7** C

Extension

Learners take it in turns to choose and read out other sentences from the story. Their classmates guess who said it.

C What's the matter? Ask and answer with a friend.

- Remind learners of the value discussion when they first read the story (see above) or discuss the value now for the first time.
- Say *Look at the picture. Who's talking?* (Zoe and a pirate) *How does Zoe feel?* (frightened)
- Say *Now look at the words in the box.* Write on the board *Are you …?* Play a miming game. Demonstrate by miming *sad*. Learners ask questions until they guess correctly (*Are you afraid? Are you sorry? Are you cold?*).
- Then in small groups, learners take turns to mime a feeling and the others guess. At the end they say *Yes, I'm feeling tired/happy/sad/excited/afraid/*etc.

Extension

Give each learner a copy of Photocopy 8 (TB page 61). Learners draw and colour tired and fine faces in the first and fourth circles to illustrate the captions. They look at the second and third faces and complete the words (*hot, angry*). They choose which names they want to complete the questions and add them.
Learners then draw their own face in the last circle and write their name next to it. They also circle all the words that describe how they are feeling now. Display their completed sheets if possible.

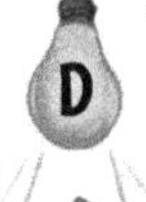

D Who was in town yesterday? Write these names around the picture on page 60. Then listen and draw lines.

- Learners copy the names above and below the picture at the bottom of page 60. Ask *How many people are in this picture?* (nine) *What are they doing?* (riding a bike, crossing the road, etc.) Ask *Can you see Zoe? What's she doing?* (going into the fancy-dress shop) *Who's she with?* (her mum)
- Say *Zoe is talking to her Uncle Hugo about the picture. Listen and draw lines from the names to the people.*

26

- Play the audio twice, pausing after *Yes! They go for a walk every day.* Ask *Who is the man in the blue trousers?* (Peter) Say *Draw a line between the man and the name Peter.* Check that learners have drawn the line correctly. Say *Now listen and draw more lines.* Play the rest of the audio twice.

Answers

Man in blue trousers with dog	Peter
Woman in yellow coat with red handbag	Lily
Girl in purple sweater with book	Clare
Boy looking at boots in shop window	Paul
Girl on bike with long blonde hair	Mary

Tapescript:

1 **Uncle:** What did you do yesterday, Zoe?
Zoe: I went to town with Mum, Uncle Hugo. We needed to get a fancy-dress costume. Here's a photo. Can you see Peter?
Uncle: The man in the blue trousers with that naughty dog?
Zoe: Yes! They go for a walk every day.

2 **Zoe:** And there's Lily. She's going to work, I think.
Uncle: The woman with the red handbag who's crossing the road?
Zoe: That's right. She's wearing her new yellow coat.
Uncle: Where does she work?
Zoe: At the hospital. She's a nurse.

3	**Uncle:**	And who's that? The little girl in the purple sweater.
	Zoe:	That's Clare.
	Uncle:	She's got a story book in her hands.
	Zoe:	That's right. She showed it to me. It's about a monster and a donkey!
	Uncle:	Ha ha!
4	**Zoe:**	That boy's name is Paul.
	Uncle:	Which boy? The one who's singing?
	Zoe:	No, the one who's looking at the boots in the window of that store.
	Uncle:	They look really cool! Did he buy some?
	Zoe:	I don't know!
5	**Zoe:**	And there's Mary. She works in a flower shop in the city centre.
	Uncle:	I can't see her. What's she doing?
	Zoe:	She's going for a ride on her bike. She's got blonde hair and it's very long and straight. She got wet in the rain.
	Uncle:	Oh dear! Did you get wet that day, too?
	Zoe:	Yes, I did!

Extension

Learners look again at the picture on page 60. In groups of three or four, learners choose five objects in the picture and write a sentence in their notebooks about each of them, using the prepositions *behind, in, on, in front of.* Write the prepositions on the board as a visual reference. Learners read out one or two of their sentences and others in the class guess what the object is, e.g. *This is in the shop window.* (bread) *These are on the tree.* (leaves)

E What do these people look like? Look, read and write.

- Say *Look at the children's fancy-dress clothes.* Ask *What can you see?* (a clown, a kitten, a doctor, a kangaroo, a pineapple, a panda, a firefighter) Ask *Which person works in a circus?* (a clown) *Which animal is black and white?* (a panda) *Which person wears a helmet?* (a firefighter) *Which person helps sick people?* (a doctor)
- Learners read the example and look at the number 1 in the box. Ask *What has sweet juice inside?* (a pineapple) Learners read the sentences and write the words on the lines. Tell them there is one extra person.
- Learners write the correct sentence number under each picture. If necessary, remind them that there will be one picture without a number.
- Learners compare their answers in pairs. Then check in open class.

Answers

2 a panda **3** a clown **4** a kitten **5** a doctor/nurse
6 a kangaroo
Pictures numbered as follows: 3, 4, 5, 6, 1, 2
The firefighter has no number.

Extension

Learners vote for the best fancy dress in the picture by putting up their hand when you say each one. Ask two learners to count the number of votes for each fancy dress so you end up with a class survey that can be summarised, e.g. *Six people liked the panda the most. Only three people liked the clown the most.*

F Which costume does Zoe want to try on? Read and complete the sentence.

- Learners find the part of the story where Zoe's mum is helping Zoe to choose her fancy dress (page 61). Learners underline the *How about* and *What about* phrases: *How about this pineapple costume? ... what about this doctor's coat?*
- Ask: *Does Zoe's mum like these clothes?* (yes) Say *She's trying to help Zoe to choose. She's giving Zoe ideas.*
- Learners look at the picture in Activity F. Ask *What are these costumes?* (a whale, an alien, a snowman)
- Learners read the conversation and underline the *How about* and *What about* phrases in it. Ask *Which fancy dress does Zoe want to try on?* (the snowman) Learners write *snowman* on the dotted line.
- Tell learners to imagine they are in a clothes shop. Say *You're with a friend in a clothes shop. Your friend wants to buy something. Help your friend.* Say *What about these jeans? How about this T-shirt?* Ask *What does your friend say?* (No, I don't like that. / No, thanks. / Yes, I like that! / Yes, that's great! / etc.) In pairs, learners practise the role play.
- Ask three or four learners *What clothes did your friend like in the shop?*

Answer

snowman

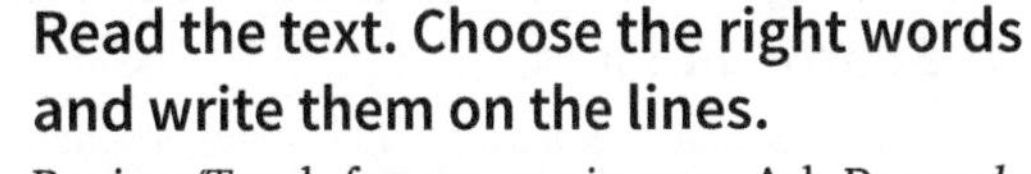

G Read the text. Choose the right words and write them on the lines.

- Review/Teach *famous, movie, map.* Ask *Do you know any famous people? Someone who is brilliant at sport or a pop star or a film star?* Learners answer. Ask *What's your favourite movie?* Show the learners a real map to teach *map.*
- Read the example together. Ask *Which word is correct?* (reading) *How many words do you write in the space?* (one)
- In pairs, learners read the sentences and choose the correct word from the group of three on the right. Check answers in open class.
- Ask more questions to check understanding. *Who was Blackbeard?* (a famous pirate) *How many pirates worked for him?* (three hundred) *How many ships did he have?* (four) *Who sailed his ship in the Red Sea?* (Long Ben) *Where can you learn more about pirates?* (on the internet)

Answers

1 But **2** who **3** worked **4** around **5** more

Extension

Learners use the text to say correct or incorrect sentences for their classmates to guess and correct, e.g. *'Whitebeard was a famous pirate.' 'Wrong!' 'Blackbeard had four ships.' 'Right!'*

Test tip: MOVERS
Reading and Writing (Part 4)

✔ When learners have chosen the word they think fits the gap, they should copy the correct word carefully because they must spell it correctly. They should never add their own choice of answer instead.

➜ Find an interesting text about animals for example and ask learners to take turns to read out a sentence each. To develop grammatical awareness, stop reading at key words and ask, e.g. *Why must we use 'these' here and not 'this'? Why must we say 'makes' and not 'make' here?* Accept answers in L1 if necessary.

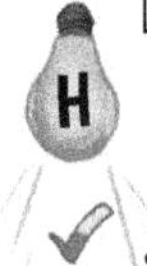

H Let's talk about books. Ask and answer with a friend. Make a diagram.

- Say *Let's talk about books.* In open class, ask different learners the questions in the four speech bubbles. Learners answer. They then take turns to ask and answer the same questions in closed pairs. Walk around and help with vocabulary if necessary.
- Different learners tell the class one of their own or their partner's answers. Prompt if necessary, e.g. *When do you / does* (Maria) *read at home?*
- Learners look at the diagram that shows information about Lucy. They draw a similar diagram with their partner's answers. Alternatively, learners draw a diagram that shows their own answers about films instead of books.

I What kind of work do they do? Find the six wrong sentences and write them in the correct places.

- Learners look at the pictures. Ask *What are these three people?* (a clown, a pirate and a nurse) *How do you spell those words? Help me write them on the board.* Learners offer spellings. Leave these three words for jobs on the board.
- In pairs, learners read the sentences that are next to the clown. Point to the sentence that is crossed out and say *This is wrong! We must move this sentence. Where can we put it?* (next to the pirate) Point to the example next to the pirate. Learners continue the activity, identifying the wrong sentences and writing them on the lines next to the correct pictures.
- Ask *Which job is the most exciting? The most difficult? The most boring?* Learners put up their hands to vote. Ask one or two learners why they think the job is exciting, difficult or boring.

Answers

The wrong ones are:

Clown:	I travel around the world on a ship. (pirate)
	I work in different parts of a hospital. (nurse)
Pirate:	I try to make people better again. (nurse)
	Come and see me at the circus. (clown)
Nurse:	In some stories, I've only got one leg! (pirate)
	People have to buy a ticket to watch me. (clown)

J Listen and write. Who is Zoe talking to?

27 IA

- Say *Listen to Zoe. She's asking one of these people some questions for her school homework.* Play the audio twice. Learners listen and write the answers. Check answers in open class.

Tapescript:

1	**Zoe:**	Excuse me?
	Woman:	Yes?
	Zoe:	Can I ask you some questions? It's for my homework.
	Woman:	OK.
	Zoe:	Thanks. What's your name?
	Woman:	My name is Elsa. You spell that E-L-S-A.
2	**Zoe:**	Do you have to work every day?
	Woman:	No. I don't work on Mondays.
	Zoe:	You don't work on Mondays?
	Woman:	No. I go swimming at the sports centre that day.
3	**Zoe:**	What must you wear when you're working?
	Woman:	I have to wear a huge red nose!
	Zoe:	A huge red nose?
	Woman:	Yes! That's right.
4	**Zoe:**	And what do you do at work?
	Woman:	I play funny and silly games.
	Zoe:	And people laugh?
	Woman:	Yes, they laugh when I play games.
5	**Zoe:**	And where do you work?
	Woman:	At the circus.
	Zoe:	Wow! That's brilliant. I love going to the circus.
	Woman:	So do I!

Answers

1 Elsa **2** Monday(s) **3** huge red nose **4** (funny and silly) games **5** circus
Zoe is talking to the clown.

- Explain, in L1 if necessary, that learners have finished the book and are ready for the Movers test. Say *Well done! Let's clap!*

8 *Let's have fun!*

Draw a fancy-dress costume and complete the text.

Ask *What would you like to wear to a fancy-dress party?* Learners tell each other in pairs. Ask two or three learners to tell the class what their partner would like to wear.

Say *Look at page 71.* Read the invitation together. Say *Draw your costume.* Working individually, learners design their fancy dress, then complete the text message answering the invitation.

Learners compare their design and their text messages.

Let's speak!

What can you wear? Ask and answer.

Say *Look at page 73, Activity 8*. Read the speech bubbles together. Ask *Where is she going?* (a party) As a class, brainstorm ideas of clothes for a party. Learners role play the conversation.

On the board write *a pirate, a doctor, a clown, a firefighter, a monster* (or other fancy-dress ideas). Say *What clothes do you need for these fancy-dress characters?* Encourage learners to suggest lots of funny ideas.

35

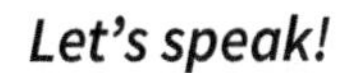

Let's say!

Say *Look at page 75, Activity 8. Listen.*
Play the audio. Learners listen.
Say *Let's say /ɜː/ Robert, curly, circus.* Repeat. Say *Tell me more English words with /ɜː/.* Learners answer (e.g. *girl, birthday, first*). Learners listen again to the audio, repeating the rhyme as fast as they can.

Home FUN booklet

Pages 6–8 and 16–17 numbers, places and directions

Picture dictionary: clothes, places, work

Go online

to practise your English
to listen to the audio recordings
to find more FUN activities!

Puppet theatre

Cut and make puppets.

2 Come to a picnic!

Plan a picnic and make a poster.

Funny sentences!

Cut and play a game.

	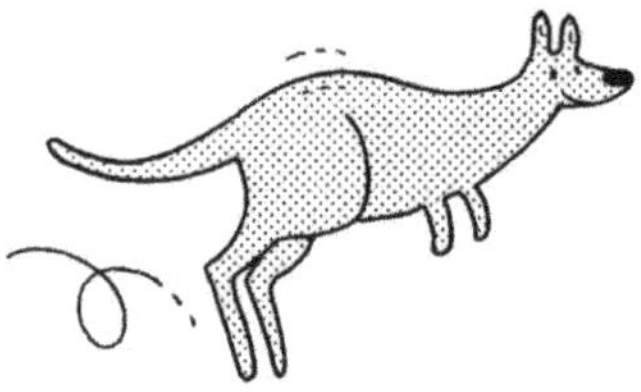	
		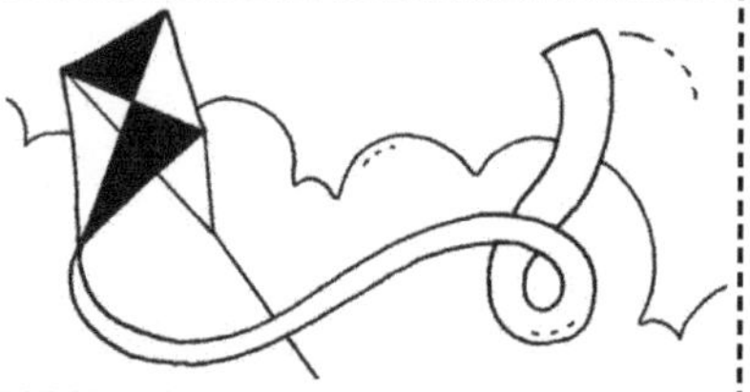
		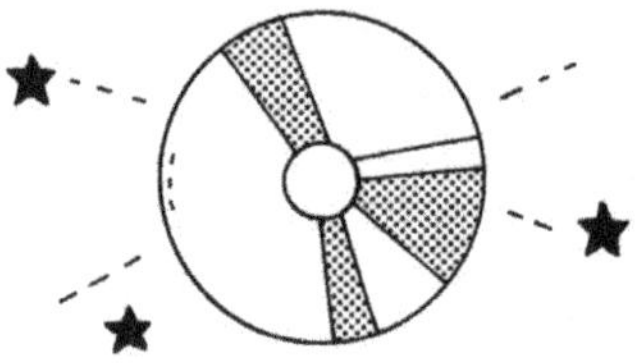
		longer
older	quieter	younger
funnier	stronger	taller
more beautiful	more boring	more exciting

My computer game

Read about the computer game.

You must move players up and down. Players can go to the shops, to the school, to the library and to the park. You must find the stars.

Now you draw a computer game page.
What must players do?

....
....
....
....

6a The funniest bodies in the world?

Draw a person's, an animal's or a monster's head or neck here.

Draw arms, hands and stomach here.

Draw legs and feet here.

6b

Which animal?

Write animal descriptions.

Draw the animals.

This animal	is	and it	can ....
			lives ....
	has		likes ....

1 This animal is yellow and brown and has lots of teeth.

2 This animal ....
....
....

3 This animal ....
....
....

4 This animal ....
....
....

5 This animal ....
....
....

6 This animal ....
....
....

7 This animal ....
....
....

8 This animal ....
....
....

7

All about clouds

Make a cloud poster.

Picture	Name	Information
	Cirrus	
	Cumulus	
	Cumulonimbus	
	Stratus	
	Nimbostratus	

What's the matter?

What's the matter, Mary?
I'm very tired!

What's the matter,
.... ?
I'm too h _ _ !

What's the matter,
.... ?
I'm very a _ _ _ _ !

What's the matter,
.... ?
Nothing! I'm fine, thanks!

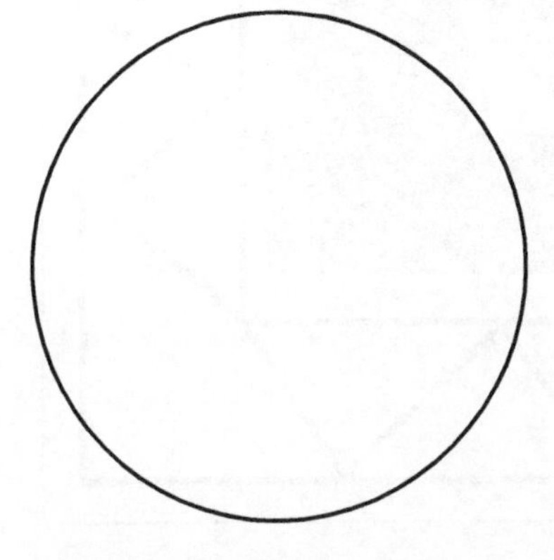

My name is .... and I'm
OK happy sad thirsty
hungry fine well angry
afraid tired hot
today!

STORYFUN
4
To: ....
Name of school: ....
Date: ....
Signed: ....
Well done!

Audio track listing

01 Title and copyright
02 Jane's clever idea
03 Jane's clever idea F
04 Jane's clever idea I
05 The perfect present
06 The perfect present H
07 The perfect present I
08 Daisy's tiger dream
09 Daisy's tiger dream C
10 Daisy's tiger dream G
11 Daisy's tiger dream H
12 A busy Monday
13 A busy Monday F
14 A busy Monday G
15 A busy Monday I
16 The tomango tree
17 The tomango tree F
18 The tomango tree H
19 Do whales have stomach-ache?
20 Do whales have stomach-ache? E
21 The grey cloud
22 The grey cloud E
23 The grey cloud H
24 The grey cloud I
25 The fancy-dress shop
26 The fancy-dress shop D
27 The fancy-dress shop J
28 Let's say! 1
29 Let's say! 2
30 Let's say! 3
31 Let's say! 4
32 Let's say! 5
33 Let's say! 6
34 Let's say! 7
35 Let's say! 8
36 Karaoke song – My bike
37 Karaoke song – The very best place

Acknowledgements

The author would like to acknowledge the shared professionalism and FUN she's experienced whilst working with colleagues during 20 years of production of YLE tests. She would also like to thank CUP for their support in the writing of this second edition of *Storyfun*.
On a personal note, Karen fondly thanks her inspirational story-telling grandfather, and now, three generations later, her sons, Tom and Will, for adding so much creative fun to our continuation of the family story-telling and story-making tradition.

Design and typeset by Wild Apple Design.

Cover design and header artwork by Nicholas Jackson (Astound).

Sound recordings by Hart McLeod, Cambridge.

Music by Mark Fishlock and produced by Ian Harker. Recorded at The Soundhouse Studios, London.

The authors and publishers acknowledge the following sources of copyright material and are grateful for the permissions granted. While every effort has been made, it has not always been possible to identify the sources of all the material used, or to trace all copyright holders. If any omissions are brought to our notice, we will be happy to include the appropriate acknowledgements on reprinting.

The authors and publishers are grateful to the following illustrators:
Key: BL = Bottom Left; BR = Bottom Right; CL = Centre Left; CR = Centre Right; TL = Top Left; TR = Top Right
Chiara Fedele (Astound) p. 54, p. 62 (TR)
Nigel Dobbyn (Beehive) p. 57
Clive Goodyer (Beehive) p. 61
Wild Apple Design p. 55
Chiara Buccheri (Lemonade) p. 62 (TL)
Bill Piggins p. 62 (CL)
Javier Montiel p. 62 (CR)
Mandy Field (Phosphor Art) p. 62 (BR & BL)